DISCOVERING THE SMALLEST CHURCHES IN WALES

DISCOVERING THE SMALLEST CHURCHES IN WALES

JOHN KINROSS

Front cover: Colva, St David. © *B. Lowry*
Rear cover: Arthog, St Catherine. © *R.W. Naesmyth of Posso*

Quotation from 'Llananno' in *Laboratories of the Spirit* by R.S. Thomas (London: Macmillan, 1975) on page 91 reproduced by permission of Kunjana Thomas
© Kunjana Thomas, 2001

First published in 2007 by Tempus Publishing

Reprinted in 2008 by
The History Press
The Mill, Brimscombe Port,
Stroud, Gloucestershire, GL5 2QG
www.thehistorypress.co.uk

Reprinted in 2014

© John Kinross, 2007

The right of John Kinross to be identified as the Author of this work has been asserted in accordance with the Copyrights, Designs and Patents Act 1988.

All rights reserved. No part of this book may be reprinted or reproduced or utilised in any form or by any electronic, mechanical or other means, now known or hereafter invented, including photocopying and recording, or in any information storage or retrieval system, without the permission in writing from the Publishers.

British Library Cataloguing in Publication Data.
A catalogue record for this book is available from the British Library.

ISBN 978 0 7524 4101 6

Typesetting and origination by
Tempus Publishing Limited
Printed and bound in England.

CONTENTS

Preface	7
Author's note	8
Acknowledgements	9
Origins of the Church in Wales	10
Maps	11
The churches	15
List of illustrations	18
The smallest churches in Wales	21
Appendices	105
The Friends of Friendless Churches	105
Welsh Religious Buildings Trust	107
The Round Tower Churches Society	110
The Open Churches Trust	111
Saints and Stones Group	112
The Historic Churches Survey Database	114

St Deiniol's Library, Clwyd	115
Glossary of terms	117
Welsh glossary	120
Bibliography	123
Index of churches by place name	124
General index	126

PREFACE

The reason for this book is that my previous volume *Discovering England's Smallest Churches* covered the Welsh border without some of the more interesting churches, which, like Snead, may be in Wales but are part of the Hereford Diocese. Then there are the wonderful small churches with screens like Partrishow and Llananno – the latter beside a busy main road and once visited by the poet R.S. Thomas: 'I keep my eyes open and am not dazzled' he wrote when confronting the famous screen, comparing it with the beauty of the nearby stream.

In Anglesey there are, appropriately you might say, some angled churches like Tal-y-Llyn, recently restored by the Friends of Friendless Churches, which has restored the economical pews as they were – two pieces of plank per pew as the seat rests on the inside wall. In North Wales the interesting churches are all beside the sea and, apart from St Tanwg near Harlech, are not difficult to see. The most interesting is perhaps St Celynnin which is approached down a steep, small road and through an elaborate porch with bell above. The inside is a surprise. Like St James, Midhopestones, near Sheffield, it has pews with names of local dignitaries. This does not mean that they sat on these pews but rather that they paid for them in the first place, rather like our brick system when we pay for a brick and add our signature to it before it is put in place.

In Pembrokeshire there are yet more churches owned by the Friends, like St Andrew, Bayvil, near Cardigan, where there is a wonderfully simple Georgian interior yet no candle holders or lighting of any kind, so that if there is a service it has to be in summer. It would be easy to leave out St Govan's Chapel, which is in good condition for a ruin, so much so in fact that it is a pity it cannot be used say once a year for a special service.

For tourists wishing to see these churches (where possible I have given key information), there are at least three weeks required and we used Hereford for the border churches as a centre, Tenby for south-west churches and Dolgellau for the north. Cadw have been most helpful, especially the staff at Rug Chapel and Bangor Diocese, who should be congratulated on their most useful loose-leaf church directory.

John Kinross
Hereford

AUTHOR'S NOTE

What constitutes a small church, you may well ask? I have used a maximum of 30ft nave and seating for 50 or less. There are a few exceptions like Pilleth, surrounded by a battlefield and recently restored. All churches in the book have been visited and those I failed to get into have been omitted. All ruins have been left out – I think St Govan's Chapel is too important and its structure too good at present to be considered a ruin – and I prefer churches with at least one service a year to those that are never used.

ACKNOWLEDGEMENTS

Thanks to the many people who have unlocked church doors for me, especially Captain Salmon on Anglesey, Glenys Morgan in Monmouthshire, the staff of Llantwit Major Church Office, Glamorgan, Ann Eastham in Pembrokeshire (author of *Saints of Stones*) and Julian Orbach (part author of Pevsner's *Pembrokeshire*). Special thanks to Bernard Lowry, who accompanied me on many forays into Powys and took many of the photographs, Matthew Saunders of the Friends of Friendless Churches, who gave me valuable notes on their Welsh churches, the staff of St Deiniol's Library, Clwyd, who found the right shelves for me and to Sallyann who typed the manuscript.

Thanks are due to my publisher Peter Kemmis Betty for his encouragement, to Alison Poole for her drawings, to John Vigar, John Taylor (maps), Rev. K. Ewen and Rev. N. Morris of the Rural Theology Association (Marches Group), to Kunjana Thomas for permission to reproduce his late father's poem 'Llananno' and finally to my wife for, amongst many other things, holding the end of the tape measure.

Finally, thanks to the late F. Claybrooke for his beautiful drawings on pages 39 and 44. I have one framed of Swansea St Anne (blue coloured) in my study.

ORIGINS OF THE CHURCH IN WALES

The disestablishment of the Church in Wales was a long drawn-out affair. After the success of the Irish Disestablishment Act in 1869, Wales was keen to follow suit. Prime Minister Gladstone was an ardent Anglican and all bills of disestablishment were thrown out. The Church meanwhile had two defenders: Bishop Edwards of St Asaph and Bishop Owen of St David's. The fall of the Liberals in 1895 pushed the question aside for many years and their return in 1905 raised the question once more. A Royal Commission of 1906 found that 74 per cent of Anglicans in Wales were nonconformists, so in 1914 an act of Parliament partly disestablished and disendowed the Church but nothing was finalised until after the First World War. A total of £4 million was sequestered of endowment money, two thirds going to county councils and one third to the University of Wales and the National Library at Aberystwyth. Lloyd George, after the war, saw through a Welsh Temporalities Act authorising payment of £1 million to the Church to make up for some of the sequestered finances. The Church in Wales got going at last on 31 March 1920 with Edwards as its first Archbishop and in 1921 the Monmouth diocese was founded; two years later the diocese of Swansea and Brecon emerged. The traditional ties between the Church and the Conservative party have lessened and the alliance between nonconformists and Church in Wales clergy has increased.

MAPS

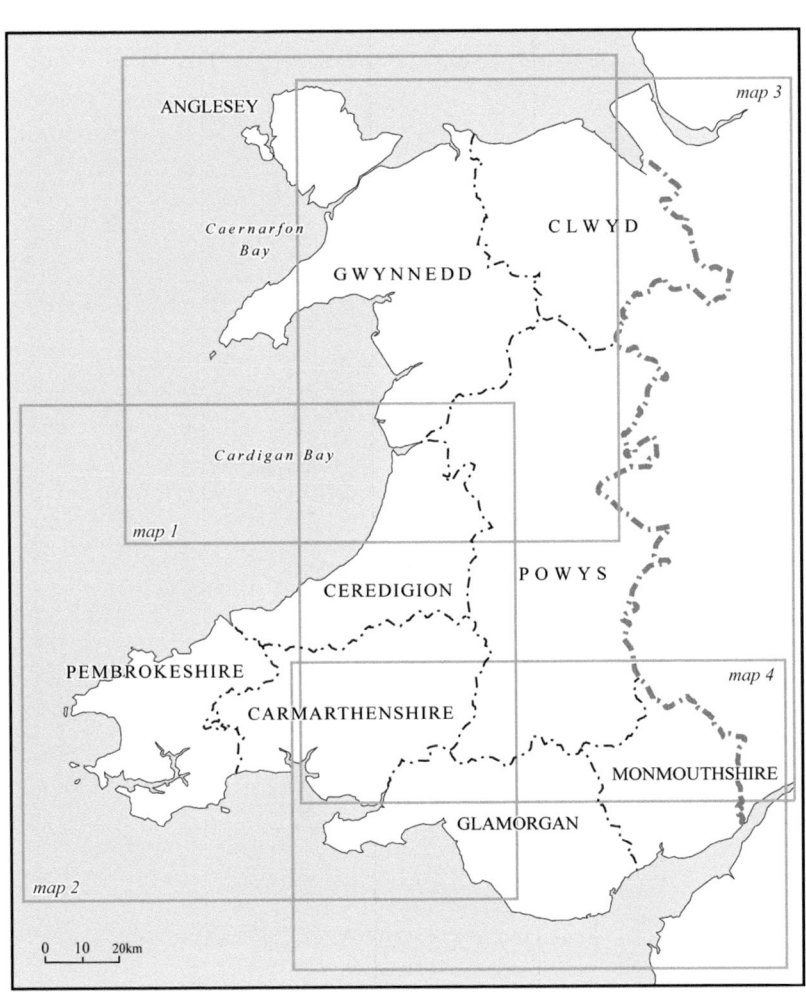

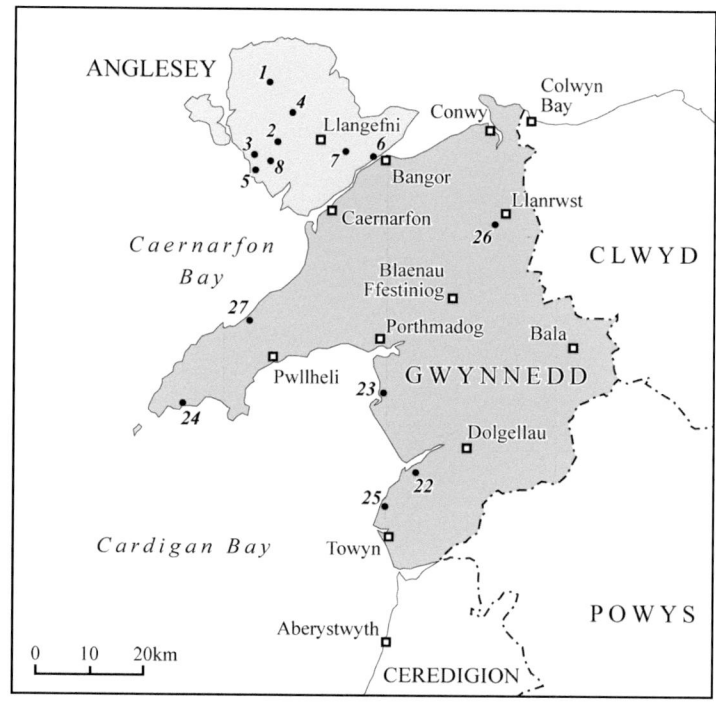
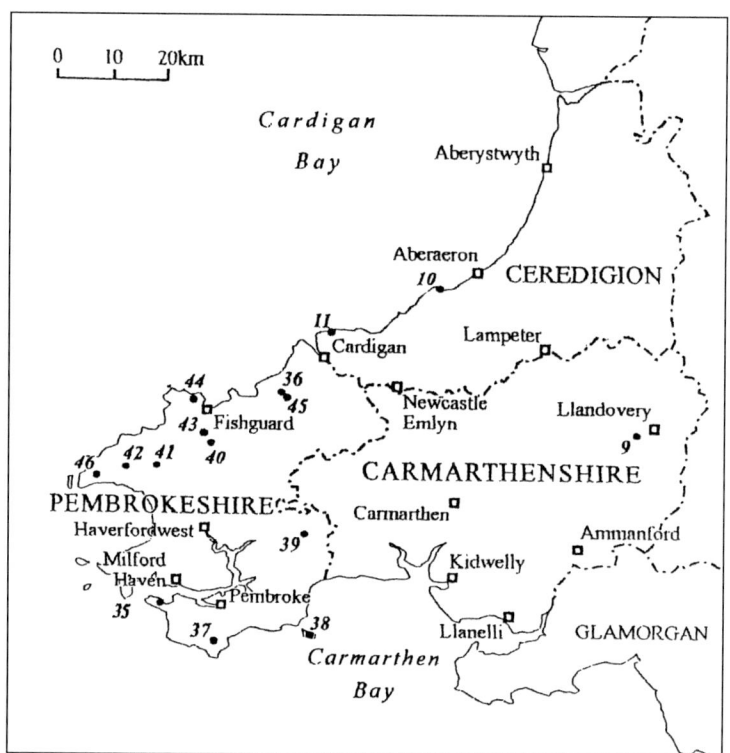

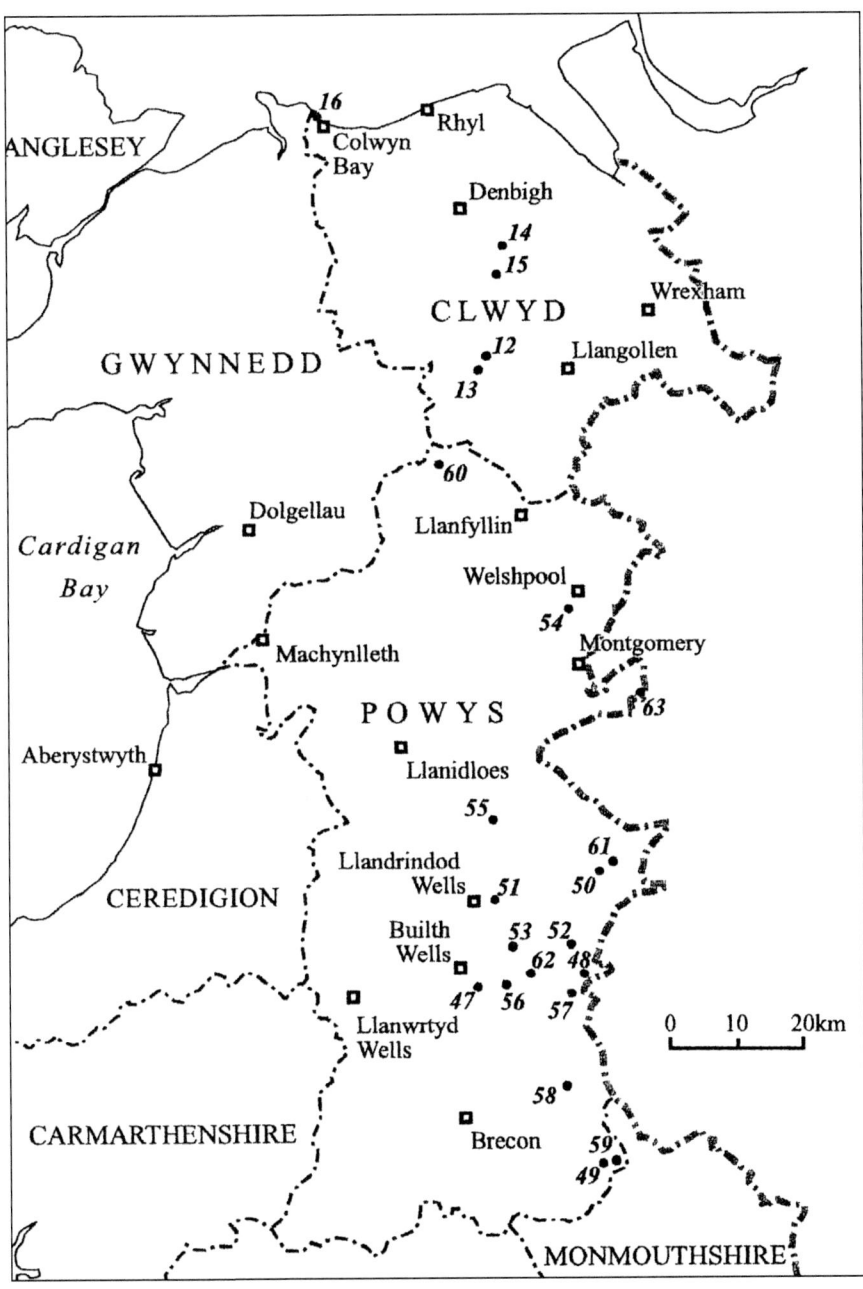

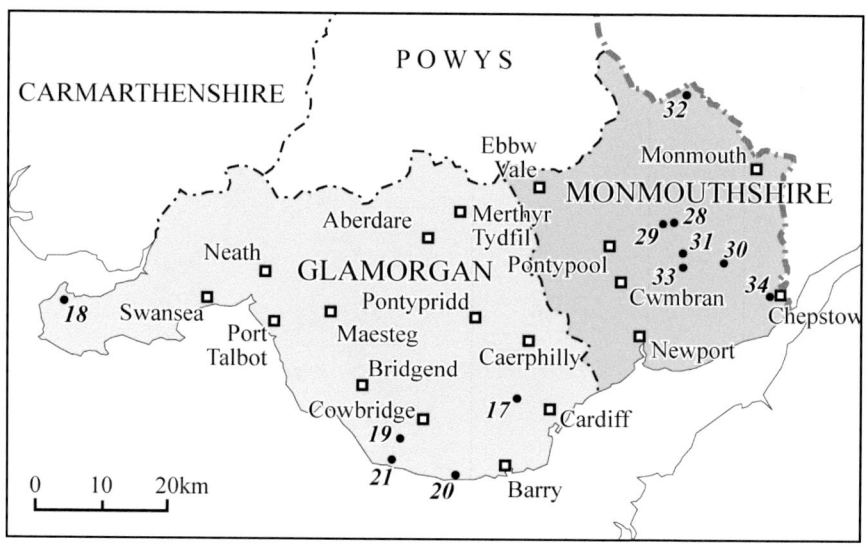

THE CHURCHES

ANGLESEY

1 Llanbabo, St Pabo
2 Llanbeulan, St Peulan
3 Llanfigel, St Figel
4 Llanfaelog, St Maelog
5 Llangwlyfan, St Cwyfan
6 Menai Bridge, St Tysilio
7 Penmynydd, St Gredifael
8 Tal-y-Llyn, St Mary

CARMARTHENSHIRE

9 Y-Strad-Ffin, St Paulinus

CEREDIGION

10 Llanina, St Ina
11 Mwnt, Holy Cross

CLWYD

12 Corwen, Rug Chapel
13 Corwen, Langar, All Saints
14 Efenechtyd, St Michael & All Angels
15 Llanhychan, St Hychan

16 Rhos-on-Sea, St Trillo

GLAMORGAN

17 Llandeilo Talybont, St Teilo (St Fagans)
18 Llanmadoc, St Madoc (Gower)
19 Llanmihangel, St Michael & All Angels
20 Porthkerry, St Curig
21 St Donats, St Donat

GWYNEDD

22 Arthog, St Catherine
23 Llandanwg, St Tanwg
24 Llanfaelrhys Rhiw, St Maelrhys
25 Llangelynn, St Caelynnin
26 Llanrwst, Gwydir Uchaf Chapel
27 Pistyll, St Beuno

MONMOUTHSHIRE

28 Bettws Newydd (no dedication)
29 Kemeys Commander, All Saints
30 Kilgrrwg, Holy Cross
31 Llangeview, St David
32 Llangua, St James
33 Llanllywel, St Ilywel
34 Mounton, St Andrew

PEMBROKESHIRE

35 Angle, Fishermen's Chapel
36 Bayvil, St Andrew
37 Bosherston, St Govan's Chapel
38 Caldey Island, St David
39 Crinow, St Teilo
40 Little Newcastle, St Peter
41 Llandeloy, St Eloi

42 Llanhowell, St Hywel
43 Llanstinan, St Justinian
44 Llanwnda, St Gwyndaf
45 Meline, St Dogfael
46 St Davids, Our Lady and St Non Chapel

POWYS

47 Alltmawr, St Mauritius
48 Bettws Chapel, Holy Trinity
49 Capel-y-Ffin, St Mary
50 Cascob, St Michael
51 Cefnllys, St Michael
52 Colva, St David
53 Cregrina, St David
54 Dolobran, Friends Meeting House
55 Llananno, St Anno
56 Llanbadarn-y-Garreg
57 Llanddewi Fach, St David
58 Llanelieu, St Ellyw
59 Partrishow, St Issui
60 Pennant Melangell, St Melangell
61 Pilleth, St Mary
62 Rhulen, St David
63 Snead, St Mary the Virgin

LIST OF ILLUSTRATIONS

MONOCHROME FIGURES

1. St Pabo, Llanbabo
2. St Peulan, Llanbeulan
3. Font at St Peulan
4. St Figel, Llanfigel, cupboard font
5. St Tysilio, Menai Bridge
6. St Mary, Tal-y-Llyn
7. Altar and rails at St Mary
8. St Ina, Llanina
9. Rug Chapel, Clwyd
10. Efenechtyd, Clwyd
11. Wooden font at Efenechtyd
12. St Hychan, Llanychan
13. Arts & Crafts porch at St Hychan
14. St Madoc, Llanmadoc, Gower
15. St Madoc – note wood carving on right and on altar
16. St Michael, Llanmihangel
17. St Donat's church and Castle
18. Buck's Print of Bradenstoke Priory nr Chippenham
19. St Anne's, Swansea, tin church
20. St Catherine's Arthog
21. Horse bier at St Celynnin, Llangelynnin
22. Gwydir Uchaf Chapel
23. Bettws Newydd church
24. Screen at Bettws Newydd and rood
25. St David, Llangeview
26. Square font at Llangeview
27. Screen at Langeview

LIST OF ILLUSTRATIONS

28 St James, Llangua
29 Altar and Candle lighting, Llangua
30 St James, Llangua
31 Old algae-encrusted tombstone, Llangua
32 St Llywel, Llanllywel
33 St Andrew, Bayvil, bier and triple-decker pulpit
34 St Govan's Chapel
35 St David's, Caldey Island
36 St Peter, Little Newcastle
37 Screen made at Cheltenham, St Eloi, Llandeloy
38 St Hywel, Llanhowel
39 St Justinian, Llanstinan
40 St Justinian, altar
41 St Gwyndaf, Llanwnda
42 St Dogfael, Label Stops
43 St Dogfael, Meline
44 Chapel of Our Lady & St Non, St Davids
45 St Mauritius, Alltmawr
46 Holy Trinity, Bettws
47 Screen and altar at Holy Trinity
48 Holy Trinity, Bettws from the east
49 St Michael, Cascob
50 St Michael and sheep
51 St Michael, roof and screen
52 St Michael, Cefnllys; Castle Hill behind
53 St Michael before destruction
54 St Michael, after 1893 de-roofing
55 St David, Colva
56 St David, pulpit and altar
57 Memonti Mori at Colva
58 Coat of arms, Colva
59 St David, Cregrina
60 St David, screen and roof
61 Dolobran Meeting House
62 Inside Dolobran, July 2006
63 St Padarn, Llanbadarn-y-Garreg altar and faded coat of arms
64 St David, Llanddewi Fach from the field
65 St David, Llanddewi Fach
66 St Ellyw, Llanelieu
67 St Issui, Partrishow in springtime
68 Rood Screen, Partrishow
69 St Melangell, Pennant Melangell

70 St Mary, Pilleth
71 St David, Rhulen – altar with flowers
72 Chancel window, St David, Rhulen

COLOUR PLATES

1   St Tysilio, Menai Bridge, Anglesey
2   Holy Cross, Mwnt, Ceredigion
3   St Beuno, Pistyll, Llyn Peninsula
4   St Gredifael, Penmynydd, Anglesey
5   Gronw Tudor and his wife at St Gredifael
6   St Cwyfan, Llangwyfan
7   St Mary, Pilleth, Powys
8   Holy Well at Pilleth
9   Candle lighting at Llanddewi Fach
10 St Peulan, Y-Strad-Ffin
11 St David, Rhulen
12 St Issui, Partrishow, Powys
13 Screen at St Anno, Llananno
14 St Ina, Llanina, Ceredigion
15 St Catherine, Arthog
16 Altar at St Teilo, Llandeloy, Pembrokeshire
17 Angle, Fishermen's Chapel
18 St Trillo, Rhos-on-Sea
19 St Govan's Chapel, Pembrokeshire
20 New Hatchment, St Mary the Virgin Snead
21 St Michaels, Cefnllys, Powys
22 St Padarn, Llanbadarn-y-Garreg
23 St Mauritius, Alltmawr
24 St Ellyw, Llanelieu, Powys
25 Screen at St Ellyw
26 St Figel, Llanfigel, Anglesey
27 St Teilo's church at St Fagans Museum

THE SMALLEST CHURCHES IN WALES

ANGLESEY

There are eight churches in Anglesey here. First call should be made to St Maelog, Llanfaelog, to obtain the useful *Bangor Directory of Open Churches*, then armed with keys one can see nearby St Cwyfan on the beach, St Figel with its wondrous seating arrangements, St Pabo and its carving, St Mary's and St Peulan. On your way back to the bridge, you can see St Gredifael with the Tudor monuments. Lastly, little St Tysilio must not be forgotten.

St Pabo, Llanbabo
After seeing St Figel, Llanfigel, the road meanders round to a large reservoir and by its banks is the small church of St Pabo, Llanbabo. The *Directory of Bangor Open Churches* gives a useful telephone number for obtaining a key. It is medieval and a typical single-cell Welsh church with windows all different and above the door three faces, with one inside. The east wall was probably rebuilt and there is a strange blocked narrow door in the north wall. Was this a leper niche and window? Today it has been reconverted into a window.

The most interesting item in this little church is the large stone carving of St Pabo. It is set up against the north wall but was discovered by a sexton digging a grave in about 1680. Lewis Morris, an eighteenth-century antiquarian, discovered that it was not made of local stone and was important enough to be set up inside the church. King Pabo is shown on the stone as bearded, crowned, and dressed in a robe, holding a sceptre with the words 'Hic Iacet Pabo Post Prud …' beneath and the rest alas broken by the sexton. Pabo was a prince of North Britain who was known as the 'Pillar of Britain' – Post Prydain. Driven out of the north in AD 460 he came to Anglesey and devoted himself to religion. His son, Dynawd Fyr became one of King Arthur's knights and, according to Wheldon Thomas, Dynawd was the father of Deiniol and it was Pabo who actually founded the monastery at Bangor (by Menai). Pabo also claimed relationship with the Empress

1 St Pabo, Llanbabo. © *Author*

Helena, mother of Constantine the Great and a saint in her own right. The island fortress where Napoleon spent his last five years is named after her.

The oldest saint on Anglesey, St Pabo is the only one we can actually picture from this amazing old stone, even if it is a thirteenth-century artist's impression of the saint.

Burglars removed the churchyard gate but the caretaker was able to get the local blacksmith to make a replacement based on the wedding photograph of his daughter and son-in-law fortunately taken standing behind the 1836 gate (not in front of it). The ruined cottage opposite was the home of Mr Jones, churchwarden. The warden's grandson is the famous inventor, Dr Jones, who gave us the breathaliser.

St Peulan, Llanbeulan

This is a closed church in the hands of the Friends of Friendless Churches and is not in the Bangor handbook. It can be found at 372755 within hearing distance of the new Holyhead road but down a grass raised walkway.

L-shaped, it is famous for its unusual font, which is twelfth century and rectangular. There is carving on three sides, one side has a cross and what appears to be two bee skeps. The other two sides have patterns and the fourth is blank.

The pews are seventeenth century and one has 'The seat of William Bold, Treyrddol Rownds 1792' on it presumably to stop anyone else sitting there. On the wall is a monument to John Williams High Sheriff, 1806. The altar is missing and one hopes will be replaced with a stone one.

2 St Peulan, Llanbeulan. © *Author*

3 Font at St Peulan. © *Author*

4 The cupboard font, St Figel, Llanfigel. © *Author*

St Peulan was a sixth-century saint. He was a disciple of St Cybi. His sister Gwenfaen was patroness of Rhoscolyn and his brother Gywngenau had a chapel at Holyhead.

St Figel, Llanfigel
Not far from Valley (where the key is kept at the local undertakers) is the small church of St Figel, Llanfigel, which is only used today for the occasional wedding and funeral.

Inside it is one of the most interesting in Anglesey. The seating is early eighteenth century. There are benches (as at Tal-y-Llyn) for the workers, space behind them for paupers to stand, two box pews for the farmers, a double pulpit on the north wall with candle holders and a bench in front for the sexton, who sometimes had to use dog-tongs to prevent dogs fighting in the service. The altar table has its side against the wall so the priest could stand sideways on and see his congregation. The two box pews left and right of the altar were for communicants. The high altar rails kept out the dogs and the squire's box pew was next to the pulpit but, apart from a few cushions perhaps, was no different from those of the farmers.

There are three fonts in the church, one is on its side, one was saved from a church taken down to build Valley airfield and the third is an unusual cupboard font set into the west wall and dating probably from about 1840. They were usually used in house chapels and often concealed inside a cupboard.

The outside bell rope is missing and it seems the original one was made of straw. A story tells how a young farmer, returning from the pub one day in the dark, heard the bell ringing and when he investigated he collided with a damp piece of rope so he fled, chased by a ghost, all the way home. When it became light, he returned and soon realised that a young bullock had entered the graveyard, eaten the straw rope and pulled the bell at the same time, then only a strand remained it could no longer reach.

By the gate is a stone stile used for unconsecrated funerals and if the light is right, you may see a carved cross on its upright stone.

St Maelog, Llanfaelog

This church is too large for this book, but worth seeing for the modern twenty-first-century updating by architect Adam Voelcker, wood carving by Colin Pearce, engraved glass 'tree-of-life' by Bill Swann and a window by Tiffany Tate.

The twelfth-century font from Tal-y-Llyn has been put here in a tree stump with uplighting and the church is a must for those who like modern church architecture.

Ask at this church to get the keys of Tal-y-Llyn, of St Peulan, Llanbeulan and to find out about the opening times of St Cwyfan, Llangwyfan – the church on the beach. The warden will also sell you a copy of the *Bangor Directory of Open Churches*.

St Cwyfan, Llangwyfan

Approached from Abberfraw where the lane bends past the church there and down to the sea. The visitor needs to cross at low tide and the church is locked most of the time. (Ask at St Maelog's for opening times.) It is a rough walk over a rocky causeway and up steep steps. Dating from the eleventh century, it once had an extra aisle. There is a tombstone near the door to a young Londoner drowned in a shipwreck.

St Cwyfan's is a favourite place for artists and photographers but at times it can be noisy as there is a car speed track nearby and the jets from RAF Valley are often overhead.

Cwyfan was a Breton, son of Brwyno and Camell. Little is known of him but at Llangyfan in Clwyd he has a church dedicated to him and a well at Diserth (supposed to cure warts).

St Tysilio, Menai Bridge (Gwynedd)

This little church can be reached by a footpath over a short causeway in the middle of the Menai Straits. It dates from the early fifteenth century and is usually locked in winter but open in summer. Like Mwnt the door is rectangular but set in a pointed doorway. The whole building was restored in the 1890s and the east window dates from 1896, the makers being Jones & Wallis of London.

5 St Tysilio, Menai Bridge. © *David Senogles*

The font, octagonal, dates from the fourteenth century and each side of the altar are the commandments and the creed so that a service can be held without any books.

St Tysilio was a younger son of Brochwel, a prince of Powys, and in the sixth century he founded a mother church at Meifod with the help of an anchorite called Gwyddfarch from Mathrafal. Tysilio's brother Cynan was beaten in battle at Chester by the Saxons and it may have been at this time that he set up his church on this tiny island.

The late David Senogles has written an excellent guide book to the history of the parish which includes the bridges, wrecks and much interesting information. For example, animals were taken over the straits at low tide and pigs swam over, for one of the little islands is Yny-y-Moch or Pig Island.

St Gredifael, Penmynydd

This is a church worth seeing for its Tudor connections. To find it, collect the key from the vicar of Llanfairpwllgwyngyll (know locally as LlanfairPG) who lives close to the BP garage. The church is next to the manor house and is dedicated to a sixth-century saint, Gredifael, who comes from a large family of saints.

Inside it looks mostly Victorian but it has a fourteenth-century font, a silver tazza (1573), a silver chalice donated by Coningsby Williams, a Tudor descendant, and dog-tongs all pictured in the guide.

The chapel has the stone ornaments of Gronw Tudor in armour and his wife Myfanwy 1385. His sword is missing and both are badly chipped but with the window showing a Tudor rose embodying both red and white roses of York and Lancaster – it is indeed a historic place. Gronw, a friend of the Black Prince, was drowned in Kent in 1382 shortly after being appointed Constable of Beaumaris

Castle. He had four brothers, one of whom was Maredudd, father of Owen Tudor. On the death of King Henry V, Owen married Katherine de Valois, Henry's widow and sister of the French king.

They had two sons, Edmund and Jasper. Edmund married Margaret Beaufort and escaped to France and their son, Henry Richmond, became King Henry VII. The unfortunate Owen took part in the battle of Mortimer's Cross (1461) on the Wales/Herefordshire border where he was captured. A plaque in Hereford marketplace marks the place where he was executed.

St Mary, Tal-y-Llyn

Not far from Holyhead and by itself on a hill, is the chapel-of-ease to the parish church of Llanbeulan. It has recently been restored by the Friends of Friendless Churches and dates from the twelfth century. The plan is L-shaped with a seventeenth-century wing chapel, which is unused at the present.

There was serious vandalism in 1990 but the Friends have rebuilt the plank pews, using the one remaining pew from 1786 as a model. The communion rails are of the same period and the altar table is painted blue which goes well with the stone flagged floor. There are triple lancet windows at the east end and a font – not the original – that dates from the fifteenth century, which has a roll moulded base and is set on an octagonal stem.

6 St Mary, Tal-y-llyn. © *Author*

7 Altar and rails at St Mary. © *Author*

St Mary's is used once a month, May to October for a 3.30pm service every third Sunday. For details about other opening times, contact the churchwarden on 01407 810448.

The Friends also own St Afran, Ieuan and Sanan at Llantrisant which looks unloved and stands in a hollow by a cow field. It is also L-shaped, and is surrounded by a full graveyard, ruined cottages and a farm. In 1899 a new church was built of easier access but lacking the charm and spirituality of the old church.

CARMARTHENSHIRE

Carmarthenshire has only one church here. It is way up a valley next to a bird sanctuary.

St Paulinus, Y-Strad-Ffin
This little church, founded in 1117 was rebuilt in 1821 by Lord Cawdor and again in 1900 by Earl Cawdor. The Cawdors – the same family as Shakespeare's Thane of Cawdor or Macbeth – were land owners in this area with houses in Stackpole, Pembrokeshire and at Golden Grove in Carmarthenshire. To reach the church, take the road from Llandovery up the valley to Cilycwm, where the key can be collected from the vicarage, then follow the RSPB signs for about 6 miles until you find the roofed lychgate and the church.

Inside it is very plain, seating – on 18 benches – about 60 and up on the roof of the internal vestry is a bier. There is an outside bell and a service about once a year. The churchyard is full, and the last grave appears to be dated about 2001. One hopes that the building will be put to good use, perhaps with support from the birdwatchers next door. This is a wonderful spot and it would be a shame to close it down.

St Paulinus, according to David Farmer, is the same person as Paul Aurelian who travelled from Wales to Brittany in the sixth century and became Bishop of Paul-de-Leon. In Wales he lived as a hermit near Y-Strad-Ffin and founded a monastery at Llanddeusant. In a field called Pant-y-Polion at Maes Llanwrthal farm, Caio, was found a stone in three pieces in the seventeenth century which was taken to Carmarthen Museum. It has the latin inscription on it which, when translated, reads: 'Preserver of the Faith, constant lover of his country, here lies Paulinus, the devoted champion of righteousness.' There are other stones found in Wales that mention Paulinus whose feast day is 12 March but sometimes he gets confused with Paulinus of York who died in October, AD 644. The two are not connected and Paulinus is very much a Welsh saint from Carmarthenshire even if his relics are resting in St Paul-de-Leon Cathedral.

It is on record that Paulinus was one of the instructors of the young St David at Ty-Gwyn in Whitland. He is supposed to have lived until he was 103.

CEREDIGION

Ceredigion has two very special churches: St Ina is worth tracking down next to its tide mark and was very spruce and tidy when we called; Mwnt, Holy Cross, is unique and has a real atmosphere. I first came across it in 1974 when exploring Fishguard and it is still a delight to see it again.

St Ina, Llanina, New Quay

To find this church, take the coast road from Fishguard towards Aberystwyth and a few miles before Aberaeron turn left at the Llanina Hotel (yellow) and proceed on the B434 towards New Quay. Just after the 30mph limit sign, turn right for about half a mile until you reach a narrow bridge. The church is before the bridge on the left in the grounds of Llanina Manor.

The church is long and narrow, 100yds from the high water mark, and seats 60. Inside it is very plain, early Victorian, with an octagonal font and an unusual fifteenth-century rood beam in the wrong place. It was rebuilt in 1850 and restored in 1905 and is thought to be the seventh church on this site. There is a delightful 1771 diagonal monument to J. Lloyd of Llanarth. The bellcote is chimney-like and there are 2.30pm services every Sunday.

8 St Ina, Llanina.
© *Author*

St Ina is a West Country saint. He was king of Wessex and, as shown in the east window, was sailing past when a storm came up so he landed here to shelter and built the church. He was the founder of Glastonbury Abbey and abdicated in 726 in favour of King Ethelred. His Saint's Day is 7 February. In the manor house lived Captain Longcroft, an excise officer, and later it became part of the Howard de Walden Estate. The area had a reputation for smuggling so the captain was kept busy.

The east end outside has a large yellow navigation mark so that any plans to enlarge this church would be difficult. The addition of an extra aisle would be expensive and would mean that the chancel would have to be enlarged too, so that one hopes it will remain as it stands, one of the delights of Ceredigion.

Holy Cross, Mwnt

Not far from Cardigan and by the sea, Mwnt's little church, whitewashed and standing alone, is certainly my favourite Welsh small church. It usually seems to be open and, even in midsummer like an August Saturday, the cars are kept well away by the National Trust Warden. There is a field of red clover, mole hills and sand to cross, a little gate and then you are in a holy place. The nave and chancel are all one, there is a parquet floor replacing the original earth floor, and the remains of the screen are on the north wall. There are seats for 45 and a regular service. Only the restored windows do not look quite right, but no doubt this building needs as much daylight as it can get in the winter.

The Flemings came to Mwnt in 1155 and there was a battle here in January, still known as Bloody Sunday. There used to be a big cross on the little hill by the church but it has vanished, probably in a storm.

CLWYD

The Cadw church and chapel (Rug and Llangar) can be seen together as only with the guide will you get into Llangar. The two churches, St Michael and All Angels and St Hychan, are respectively south and north of Ruthin, while little St Trillo is on the beach at Rhos-on-Sea which is almost part of Colwyn Bay.

Rug Chapel (Denbighshire)
Strangely this important chapel does not appear in the Clwyd edition of the Pevsner series. However, the chapel, just north of the A5 near Corwen, is in the safe hands of Cadw, who publish a combined guide book containing Rug, Llangar church nearby and Gwydir Uchaf Chapel at Llanrwst.

9 Rug Chapel, Clwyd. © *Author*

Rug is only open Wednesday to Sunday in the summer months, when the curator runs a tour of nearby Llangar at 2.00pm for the same ticket. Gwydir is 25 minutes away and the key is kept at Gwydir Castle, where the guide can take you over the road and up the hill to see inside the seventeenth-century building with its painted ceiling.

From the outside, Rug looks like a Victorian building, for it was mostly rebuilt in 1854, and with its rather prim garden and lavender bushes it is a great surprise to go inside and see a Charles I Laudian chapel with a painted roof and the date 1637 standing out on the east beam. Climb to the gallery to get a good look at this. There are carved angels, large and small, and a carved screen, partially Victorian and a lectern-pulpit which was incorporated into the screen cleverly by the restorers.

One of the surprises is the stained glass window on the north wall showing Pilate's wife and an angel: 'I have suffered many things because of him' she says. Opposite is a rather mundane window of the Rock of Ages. There is also a Welsh seventeenth-century wall painting of a reclining skeleton, hourglass and two candles depicting the transient nature of life.

There are two canopied pews flanking the altar, a seventeenth-century luxury touch, similar to St Michael's, Rycote, Oxfordshire (under the care of English Heritage). When you have seen this chapel, wait outside until 2.30pm for the guide to take you the 2 miles to Llangar.

Llangar, All Saints (Denbighshire)

Llangar is a surprise. Originally it was 'Llan-Garw-Gwynn' or the church of the white deer. A white deer was found in a thicket, the legend says, and the boundaries of the parish were decided by the direction the deer ran. It stands close to the River Dee and may well have been built on a small fortified enclosure. There had been subsidence during the seventeenth and eighteenth centuries and the small congregation struggled hard to keep the church going. In 1853 a new church was built at Cynwyd so the 1974 Cadw refurbishment was vital to save the church. Their black and white photograph shows many props holding up the barrel ceiling and the first thing the restorers had to do was dig up the floor, even now the east end is 1ft 8in higher than the West end. There are eighteenth-century box pews, a triple-decker pulpit and a gallery which has an unusual pyramidical music stand for a choir and church band. The strange thing about this is that the stand is built into a bench so the musicians would have to sit with their legs each side of the bench, or some stools would have to be carried up and there would not have been much space for them. The present font, a stone bowl, is set into the wall by the south door, although prints show it before 1732 as free-standing by the pulpit. The wall paintings are best read up in the article by A.J. Parkinson in the guide book. There is a wonderful skeleton with a pick and shovel depicting the transience of life, and animals (a fine boar) on the south wall depicting the Seven

Deadly Sins. Some of the other wall paintings are very faint and a great deal of imagination is required to interpret them.

Outside, there is an eighteenth-century stone lychgate. A cutaway reconstruction shows the north door open with a path up from the river (so the medieval congregation may have come by boat), benches along the walls, straw on the floor and the wall paintings being used to teach the congregation the difference between good and evil. They were restored in 1991.

St Michael and All Angels, Efenechtyd (Denbighshire)

The name 'Efenechtyd' seems to be a derivation from 'mynech', a monk or nun, and 'tyd' meaning 'land' or 'place'. This site may well have been associated with monks or nuns. The dedication to St Michael is apt as the old road from St Davids to Holywell passed through the hamlet and St Michael is the patron saint of travellers.

The church is entered unusually through the west door. It measures 47.5ft x 20.5ft and the nave is only 20ft from step to font. The latter, perhaps the most unusual item in the church, is made of hollowed-out oak, with a lead centre, dating from about the fifteenth century. The other font, sitting on top of a stone near the door, was once used as a drinking bowl for dogs.

10 Efenechtyd, Clwyd. © *Author*

11 Wooden font at Efenechtyd.
© *Author*

The east window is modern, decorated, and not to everyone's taste. Perhaps the most unusual item is the sawn-off screen made of oak matching the font. The Pevsner for Clwyd says it was part of the original rood screen, but the local guide book by Fletcher and Williams says that the church once had a gallery and that this was probably removed by Arthur Barker in 1873 when he carried out extensive work costing about £600, over half of which came from these people and associations:

St Asaph Church Building Society	£25
The London Incorporated Building Society	£20
Bishop Carey's Fund	£20
The Rector of Efenechtyd, Rev. John Pughe Evans	£100
Mr West, Ruthin Castle	£25
Mr Blezzard, Pool Park	£20
Mr H.P. Evans, Calcutta	£25
Lord Bagot	£25
Mrs Evans, Efenechtyd Rectory	£25
Mrs Fairclough, Efenechtyd	£20
Mrs Lloyd, Rhaggard	£10
Lord Bishop of St Asaph	£10

It is a remarkable sum to be raised for such a small church.

The monuments include one for the Conway family with the crest of a blackamoor's head. The village pub was 'The Blackamoor Inn' and there is also an old wooden monument of 1810 to Catherine Lloyd, with the margins covered in a mixture of cherubs and skull and crossbones. In Latin is a long dedication to John Walters, MA, rector in 1789 and headmaster of Ruthin School from 1785-89. In a glass-topped case is a Welsh Prayer book of 1664. Inside, in Welsh, is a recipe for gruel and in English, dated 2 July 1707, are notes on the sheep and lambs of John Roberts. Was the gruel for himself or the sheep?

Finally, there is a door knocker, shaped like a rowlock which, if grasped, would afford sanctuary in the days when such things were believed.

St Michael's has a service at 9.30am every Sunday and shares a vicar with Llanfair and Llanelidan. Until recently St Mary's Derwen was part of the group. This is off the road to Bala and has a fine screen, but is no longer used and is looked after by the Friends of Friendless Churches (see Appendix I).

Efenechtyd church is usually open in daylight hours. It has a circular llan with a large roofed lychgate and an ancient yew tree. It is well worth a visit.

St Hychan, Llanychan (Denbighshire)

This little church is close to the village of Rhewl near Ruthin. It stands close to a small river and is approached by a path through a gate. It stands next to what looks like the old rectory but was in fact the school. There is a stone mounting block on the path. Usually locked, the key can be obtained from the rector.

The church was supposed to have been founded on the site of an anchorite cell in AD 450 and St Hychan (spelled 'Hychen' in Pevsner) of Llanychan was a relation of Brychan Brychenin who came from Carmarthen. His family had property there near the present railway station.

The porch, Victorian but Arts & Crafts style, has wooden guttering and a wooden drainpipe. The only other example I have seen of this is on a cottage in Weedon, Buckinghamshire. The door is very old. Most of the building dates from the restoration by Arthur Baker in 1877-8. The striking east window dates from 1925 and was the gift of Sir Crosland Graham and his wife. Forsyth's glass shows the donors, one of whom with a moustache and a shield looks remarkably like the late post-war Prime Minister, Clement Attlee.

The organ also has carvings left and right of the console with the date 1923, and was presented by the Grahams.

There is a reset stone window of 1626 which must have come from somewhere else as it does not match up. The bell has a large wheel attached to it, usually visible from the outside. Behind the altar is a reredos made from reused timbers, which contains the quotation from I Corinthians, 11/28 (in Welsh) which reads in English: 'Let a man examine himself and so let him eat of that bread and drink of that cup.'

Above: 12 St Hychan, Llanychan. © *B. Lowry*

Left: 13 Arts & Crafts porch at St Hychan. © *B. Lowry*

The terrier in the vestry is very complete and references the mona marble font (1737), the 10 pews with brass plaques with names of local farms, the vicar's desk with unusual pine tree carving (1730) and the unusual bosses in the roof, which were made of coloured clay and look as if they were added later. The west window has the initials KRM and SMMM and the memorial to Maurice Jones has his crest on it of three boars heads with a central chevron.

The pulpit has a hole for a sandglass, an unusual item to find nowadays, dating back to long sermons when even the sermon-giver would get concerned if the sand ran out before he had finished his sermon, perhaps because he feared his Sunday roast beef would be burned before he and his wife reached home.

In 1872, St Hychan was the smallest church in the diocese and in early spring, with its mass of snowdrops, it is worth a visit.

St Trillo's Chapel, Rhos-on-Sea (Clwyd)

This is the smallest regularly used chapel in Wales, dating from the sixth century and measuring 11ft x 8ft. It is covering St Trillo's well and was originally on an island but the changing coast has placed it on the seashore. The forest that surrounded it is now in the sea and remains of the trees are sometimes washed ashore. Inside, there are six home-made seats and the weekly communion service is usually held outside in the summer months. St Trillo was a friend of St Mungo and they had a religious community on the site. His father was Hael of Llydaw.

GLAMORGAN

I have included five churches here and was influenced by the Llantwit Major church office. Llanmihangel, St Donat's and St Curig can be seen from here. The Gower church is worth a day's visit and Gower is a place to walk and picnic and another day was spent on visiting St Fagan's Museum where the outside of St Teilo's church was visible even if it was closed inside.

Llandeilo Tal-y-bont, St Teilo

This medieval church, formerly known as the 'church in the marshes' at Pontardulais, has long become a ruin, but its wall paintings have been taken down and preserved. The new St Teilo had been built in 1850 so, as so often in Wales, the clergy encouraged the congregation to attend the new St Teilo and abandon the old one. The roof came off part of this twin nave church and all looked very bleak until about 10 years ago when St Fagan's Natural History Museum expressed an interest and, with a site behind the Working Men's Institute in mind, took the church stone by stone and rebuilt it in the spacious grounds of St Fagan's, near Cardiff. Here it stands today, open to the public; the screen has been replaced, the wall paintings executed, there is a new underfloor heating system but everything else is the same. The work has been supervised by Mr Nash of the museum and the roof carving carried out by an expert who worked on the restoration of Windsor Castle after the fire..

St Teilo (later Bishop Teilo of Llandaff) is not to be confused with St Tysilio. Both have Hereford connections as the young Teilo is supposed to have been educated at Hentland – close to St Tysilio's church at Sellack. Teilo was the son of Ensic and Guenhaf and is supposed to have gone to Jerusalem with David and Padarn. During the Yellow Plague, Teilo went to Brittany where he planted the huge orchard that spread from Dol to Cai. He is forever associated with a stag in Brittany as he was offered the land he could cover in a day, so he hopped on a friendly stag and was granted a huge area. In 577 after the Battle of Deorham near Bath, when the victors crossed the Wye, King Ynyr of Gwent's son Iddon got Teilo to help rally the troops, which he did where White Castle stands. In a field called Maes-y-Groes he raised a cross as a rallying point. The invaders were beaten back.

Teilo died at Llandeilo Fawr and his famous cartulary was presented to Landaff Cathedral. There are no less than 37 churches in Wales, mostly the south, associated with him some, alas, in ruins but at least one has risen from the ashes and is available for all to see.

St Madoc, Llanmadoc, Gower

To reach this church it is easier to go round Swansea on the motorway and turn off at Exit 47, then proceed via Gowerton, Llanrhidian, Weobley Castle (worth a stop) to Llanmadoc. There are 15 churches on the Gower (an area of Outstanding Natural Beauty) connected by a Trail in the summer, but only this one is small enough for this book and that is St Madoc's at Llanmadoc. It is open Easter–October.

St Madoc or Madog founded a college at Llangenydd with his brother Cenydd on the Gower. His life follows that of Aidan and some authorities think they were one and the same person. His special day was 12 November when special pies were made at Llanmadoc of chopped mutton and currants and farmers attempted to sow their wheat before 12 November so it could lie for 40 days without sprouting. In the rectory was found a stone, probably a sixth-century tombstone, with a Latin inscription that reads 'the stone of Advestus son of Guanus. He lies here.' Was Guanus St Govan? Also a small hand-bell of Celtic origin now at Penrice Castle was found in a field near the church.

The building today dates from the Prichard reconstruction of 1865 under the direction of the incumbent, Rev. J.D. Davies, an Anglo-Catholic with a liking for Switzerland, hence the sight of the chalet rectory opposite having its roof fixed when we arrived and the wood carvings inside including the altar with its painted four panels showing Matthew, Mark, Luke and John.

14 St Madoc, Llanmadoc, Gower.
© *F. Claybrooke*

15 St Madoc – note wood carving on right and on altar.
© *Author*

Davies was visited by Francis Kilvert on 16 April 1872, with the vicar of Ilston in a 'pretty new wagonette'. They arrived to be greeted by Mr Davies, 'who looked like a Roman priest, close-shaven and shorn, dressed in seedy black, a long coat and broad shovel hat.' They found the church 'beautifully finished and adorned but fitted up in the high ritualistic style'. They ate a very good pie in the unfinished rectory which was 'thoroughly untidy and bachelor-like' and full of 'pretty wood fretwork and carved work' in the hall (the vicar's hobby) as well as the 'rigging of a boat'. They left with Rev. Davies promising to make a 10s bookcase for Francis but whether it was ever made, one doesn't know.

There are two other carved stones with crosses in the west end of the church proving that the site was very important in the history of Christianity in Wales. The font is square with a damaged curved base decoration and it is only 18ft from the chancel arch. There is a 1950 east window commemorating the lives of Mr and Mrs Bevan of Glebe Farm. It was erected by their grandchildren and shows a farmer and his wife in medieval dress bringing the fruits of their labours to Christ with, in the quatrefoil above, a cottage, sheaves and a mown field. It was made by Swansea's Celtic Studios.

Outside the tower is a small defensive structure with a crow-stepped hipped roof and there are two crosses, quite different from those on the chancel and east end of the nave roof. The vestry is under the tower (hardly any room to swing a cat) and the bell tower above used to have two bells, now alas only one, which was cast in 1675 by an itinerant bellfounder.

From Llanmadoc it is worth calling at the Pottery at nearby Cheriton to obtain the key to see the cruciform church with yet more carving by Rev. Davies.

St Michael and All Angels, Llanmihangel

St Michael is the smallest of the nine churches in the Llantwit Major team but it still has a nave just over 30ft long. Situated in a dell about 3 miles north of Llantwit Major, it is best approached via Llanmaes. If locked, the key can be obtained from the sixteenth-century manor house opposite.

It has a fortified tower, battlemented with a saddleback top and arrow loops and inside the staircase tower seems to be equipped with a chimney. There are nine oil lamps still but most services are held in daylight. The roof is late fifteenth century with an arch and wind braces and two east bays are boarded forming a celure over the rood which, although removed, still has its stone stair and openings. The corbels supporting the roof beams are all carved, three with faces.

16 St Michael, Llanmihangel. © D.V. Ginn

In the chancel are two monuments to the Edwin family. Sir Humphrey's (former Lord Mayor of London) dates from 1722. His niece was Lady Elcho (connected to Lord Elcho, Bonny Prince Charlie's cavalry commander at Culloden) and one wonders if he was a Jacobite. The other monument is to Charles Edwin (d.1777). There is also a 1591 monument to Griffith Grant which looks like a tomb lid set into the north wall. The setting makes this church worth a visit and when I first arrived I assumed there was a chapel to the left of the manor; however, but it seems it is a barn, and there is a much larger barn with seven bays, one of the largest still intact in Glamorgan.

St Curig, Porthkerry

This little church is at the Cardiff end of Rhoose Airport and outside the noise of aircraft is deafening, but inside with the door shut all is peace and quiet. If locked, the vicar's telephone number is on the board by the lychgate and the warden lives nearby.

Some of the building is thirteenth century and in the nave the south doorway is very early but the porch is Victorian and the original entrance is via the west door of the tower, now a window. There is a vestry added on to the north wall with three windows dating from 1929. The stained glass is of interest, a fine east window of St Peter and St John by Newbery (?1867), a delightful small window to St Curig (modern) and an even more delightful window in memory of John Jickells, a local teacher who must have been a butterfly enthusiast as there are 15 of them pictured (1985). One of the monuments to Reynold Portreye is a slab placed horizontally on the north wall with the lettering added vertically, rather unusual but spoilt by higgledy-piggledy additions.

Next to the organ is a photograph of the gravestone of Peter Bowen, organ pump boy in the 1930s. He joined the army and was killed at Caen, 1944. The west window shows King David and his lyre and was put there when the door was blocked.

St Curig gave up a military career and became a monk. He had a cross covered in silver and gold kept in Harmon's church in Powys. There was a pilgrimage chapel: Capel Curig, Pembrokeshire, which no longer exists. Porthkerry had a castle, destroyed by the sea, where Ceri or Longsword, built ships to defend this coast. Were Ceri and Curig the same person?

The church was once thatched but the thatch was replaced with slate and the box pews replaced by Victorian pews. Wesley preached here twice in October 1741 and there are six bells, the oldest (1550) having been recently restored by Taylors of Loughborough. It is a well cared for building like so many churches close to airports.

St Donat, St Donat's

This is slightly larger than most churches included but it has an interesting history which closely allies with the castle above (now Atlantic College) that once belonged to William Randolph Hearst.

The church is down a steep lane to the right of the castle and there is a car park at the end of the lane. It is a simple tower (defensive), nave and chancel church with an added Lady Chapel (kept locked). The original building was Norman, but smaller with an apse (c.1100) as sanctuary and the chancel arch is Norman. The Stradling family who built the castle c.1300 enlarged the church and built the tower and Lady Chapel, the latter housing their monuments. The alabaster one of Sir Edward and his wife, Agnes, facing him is very fine and nine years ago the PCC spent £27,000 restoring it. He has a Punch-like nose and his wife a new nose. The chapel, 20ft x 12ft, alas has a tomb in the middle of it and no altar, but tradition has it that one of the family was a Roman Catholic who held services there and spent two years in the Tower of London as a result. There are sixteenth-century pictures of three members of the family in the chancel (the originals are in Cardiff Museum) – one member was kidnapped by Mr Dolphin, a local pirate, but released when the latter's ship was captured off the Gower. Dolphin was tortured in the castle dungeons and presumably did not survive. Another Stradling died in a duel in France with his former friend Sir John Tyrrwhitt and during the Civil War Sir Edward, his brother and son fought for King Charles leaving Lady Stradling alone in the castle. It passed via the Tyrrwhitts of Amersham to the Carnes and the east window is a Victorian memorial to Edward Stradling Nicholl-Carne (d.1862). The south-east window shows St Peter and St Elizabeth and is dedicated to the Branckers, in-laws of J.W. Stradling-Carne who is commemorated in the south-west window showing Jesus feeding the multitude.

The porch in the tower is a magnificent affair, like a large eggcup with two rows of blank shields. In 1907 some alterations were made by Morgan Stuart Williams, owner of the castle 1901-9, including rebuilding the altar which looks more like a 1960 construction than 1907. Hearst spent a lot of money on the castle, including creating Bradenstoke Hall, which was formed out of the ruins of Bradenstoke Priory, Wiltshire, including some stained glass. The SPAB at the time (1929) were so outraged they advertised the before and after pictures on the London Underground. Hearst also took the woodwork out of Gwydir Castle dining room and the present owners had to buy it back from New York (see Gwydir Castle Chapel, p.47) In the churchyard are two calvary crosses, one modern (1878) but the other medieval, showing the Virgin Mary and Christ and on the other side a Crucifixion scene.

For photographers the best view is south of the church, where you can get the castle in as well the church, as shown in the (guide book) sketch opposite. St Donatus, it seems, was the patron saint of 'storm-tossed sailors' and he visited the church en route for Rome in c.AD 850.

17 St Donat's church and castle. *Courtesy Church Guide*

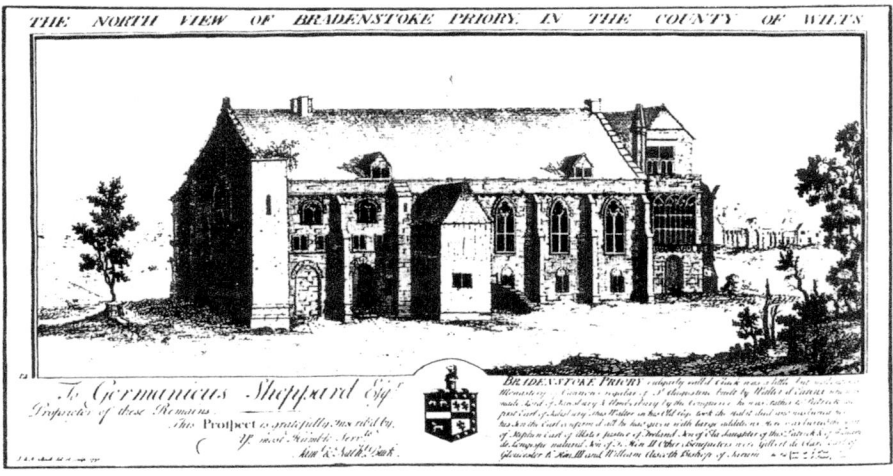

18 Buck's print of Bradenstoke Priory near Chippenham

Buck's print of 1732 shows Bradenstoke Priory near Chippenham, Wiltshire which was purchased by William Randolph Hearst in the 1920s and demolished. Some of the stained glass and other pieces were reassembled in St Donat's Castle which he also owned at that time.

TIN CHURCHES

There are several tin churches in Wales, well described by Ian Smith in his book *Tin Tabernacles*, Central Books, 2004. I have listed the small ones in Wales that are still in use as churches today; six are in Glamorgan.

Red Pisgah Mission church, Knolton Bryn, Overton, Wrexham, Clwyd
St David's church, Nebo, Nr Aberaeron, Ceredigion
St Anne's, New Hedges, Tenby, Pembrokeshire (recently repainted blue and white)
Pembroke Apostolic church, Pembroke, Pembrokeshire
St Anne's church, Penllergaer, Swansea, Glamorgan (9.15 Holy Communion on second, third and fourth Sundays)
Bethel Evangelical church, Rhoose, Glamorgan
Church of St Andrew, The Wern, Minera, Wrexham, Clwyd
Seventh Day Adventist church, Trealaw, Rhonnda, Glamorgan
United Reform church, Tredomen, Powys
St Thomas church, Pantbach Road, Cardiff, Glamorgan
Eastbrook Methodist church, Dinas Powys, South Glamorgan
Eglwysfach (small church), Nr Machynlleth, Powys (on A487)
Ganll-wyd Tin church, Dolmelynllyn, Gwynedd
Church of the Good Shepherd, Drury, (Flintshire), Clwyd
All Saints church, Pant y Grog, Glamorgan
Tin church, Pensarn, Abergele, Gwynedd (9.00am Holy Eucharist, 3.00pm Sung Eucharist on Sundays and 10.30am Holy Eucharist, Tuesdays)

There was also a tin church for Norwegian seamen in Swansea port, which has been dismantled, but will be re-erected as a Visitor Centre.
  Firms like Boulton & Paul built 'flat-pack' churches that could be transported by rail. Cooper's of Old Kent Road, London, advertised a 30ft x 20ft, 8ft eaves and 16ft ridge church for £107 10s erected complete or £77 10s packed on rail or wharf for your own erection.

19 St Anne's, Swansea, tin church.
© F. Claybrooke

GWYNEDD

We saw Gwydir Uchaf Chapel (and the castle) after visiting Rug and Llangar. Then, based at Dolgellau, we took the coast road to see Arthog and Llangelynn. Going north, we visited St Tanwg in the sand and then on the Llyn Peninsula the delightful Pistyll and the long, rather plain, Llanfaelrhys near Rhiw. We must go back and see Bardsey Island.

St Catherine's, Arthog (Merionethshire)

This is an 1830 church, small and square, on the main A493, which is easy to find but dangerous to stop at as the only parking place is in the lane opposite which may already have cars parked there.

The shape of the church is unusual as it has a gallery with circular staircase in a turret next to the porch. Both have gable roofs and round the north side is an added vestry also with a gable roof.

St Catherine of Alexandra, a fourth-century martyr, was an able girl who protested against the persecution of Christians by Maxentius. He tied her to a wheel with spikes and after this torture she was executed. She has become the patron saint of wheelwrights, scholars and attorneys and her feast day is 25 November.

The church has a Victorian east window showing shepherds and angels in memory of Thomas Taylor, Sheriff of Merioneth, 1799-1876. The round west window, dated 1951, is dedicated to a local woman, Henrietta Curr, and has flowers, barley stalks and what looks like a Masonic cross.

The lectern is a fine brass eagle and on the walls are quotations from the Psalms: 'I will lift up mine eyes unto the hill from whence cometh my help', 'Peace be within in thy walls' and 'To the Lord God belong mercies and forgiveness'.

This church is kept locked but the local warden keeps the key or it can be obtained via the rectory at Llwnygwril.

20 St Catherine's Arthog. © *PCC Newsletter* (see also back cover)

St Tanwg, Llandanwg (Merionethshire)

On the beach south of Harlech and frequently partially covered in sand, St Tanwg is the old parish church for Harlech. St Tanwg was a Breton prince who studied at Bangor and founded the church, *c.*AD 450. By legend, St Patrick came here as there was a ridge, called Sarn Badrig, that crossed the sea to Ireland – some say it is still visible at low tide. The church retains its original rood beam and two early inscribed stones; one from the fifth century is built into the east chancel window and the other, Roman, is in the south chancel window. In the nineteenth century, the church fell into disrepair and was rescued by the Society for the Protection of Ancient Buildings.

The National Trust warden who looks after the nearby car park has a key to this building which is open irregularly in the summer. The local café owner seems to know the whereabouts of the warden.

The gated, roofed porch would be convenient for pallbearers to rest in the rain but even then it must be tricky to get to the door of the church as the path round it is so narrow.

St Maelrhys, Llanfaelrhys, near Rhiw (Caernarfonshire)

After visiting Aberdaeron and the R.S. Thomas bits and pieces, the lane climbs past the church and after 2 miles arrives at the hamlet of Llanfaelrhys, Rhiw where the rectangular church stands inside a square walled churchyard. There are steps and a mounting block at the west end of the south wall. There are some box pews on the south and benches on the north side with seating for 70. Nave and chancel are all one, measuring 57ft 10in x 14ft. There were early north and south doorways and the centre of the church is medieval. Later, and with thinner walls, the east end was extended and in the nineteenth century the west end was also extended to give double vestries and an inner double door. The windows were replaced about this time.

The font is fifteenth century, just an octagonal stone bowl on a splayed base like a chess pawn upside down. Everything is plain and simple, there are no kneelers and there is a monument to Dr Robert Owen, deceased 1892, aged 23. There are also seven brass plaques.

St Maelrhys came to Wales with St Cadfan and was probably buried in nearby Bardsey Island.

> **BARDSEY ISLAND**
>
> In Wales the island is also known as Ynys Enlli – the island of currents – and the ruined walls of St Cadfan's monastery still stand. Boat trips run in the summer by Tony Bruce from Pwllheli and nearby Porth Meudwy. It is essential to book but it is best to contact the Bardsey Island Trust first if the weather is doubtful. The trip takes about 15 minutes from Porth Meudwy with 3.5 hours on the island, Sunday to Friday and over an hour at sea from Pwllheli. There is a shop and some self-catering accommodation and it is a popular destination for birdwatchers.

St Celynnin, Llangelynnin (Merionethshire)

The first I heard of this interesting old church was by its calendar hanging on the wall of our rented cottage in Dolgellau. It is sited near Towyn between the cliff railway and the cliff road and there is a steep walk down to its walled enclosure. There is a large bell inset into the south porch (1842). The benches in the nave are all named, not by users, but by local land owners who have entitled seats (1823), and indicate that the back bench is for the 'others'. There is a screen of sorts and the church is used regularly. The slate roof has recently been repaired and the west end has a pronounced berm to help with possible land slippage. At the entrance to the porch is a stone marking the grave of Abram Wood (1799) who was king of the Welsh gypsies.

On the wall is a unique two-horse bier. This operated with two same-height horses, nose to tail, with a special harness and the coffin would have to be firmly strapped on so that it did not slip sideways, backwards or forwards. The undertakers presumably had an experienced horseman, perhaps a retired drover, to cope with the journey, which would have been perhaps easier up hill than down. The progress must have been very slow and for outlying farms must have taken most of the day.

Gwydir Uchaf Chapel, Llanrwst (Caernarfonshire)

Founded in 1673 by Sir Richard Wynn, this chapel stands above Gwydir Castle and the guide book shows it as fully furnished with 12 seventeenth-century high-back chairs and a gate-legged altar table. Alas, all chairs plus the altar table have been locked up by Cadw. The Wynn family also have a chapel attached to the local church in Llanbedr.

Smaller than Rug and Llangar, the first thing that strikes you on entering Gwydir Uchaf is the baroque painted ceiling with angels. There are matching angels carved out of flat wood at the foot of each arched roof beam. They have the words in Latin of the hymn used at Vespers, 'Veni Sancte Spiritus et Reple Corda Fidelium' (Come Holy Spirit and fill the hearts of the faithful …) in their hands.

21 Bier at St Celynnin, Llangelynnin. © *Author*

22 Gwydir Uchaf Chapel. © *Author*

This was a High Anglican chapel and may account for the castle having priest holes. The musician's gallery has stout, painted balusters decorated by roundels and rectangles painted red and gold on the pale blue woodwork. There is some fine panelling and there are carved wooden figures on the pulpit. Behind the pulpit is the Charles II coat of arms.

Judy Corbett and her husband (who own the castle now) were married here and her book *Castles in the Air* describes the marriage. Her dog sat on her train, and was described as the bridesmaid, and she had troubles with her dress. 'Gwydir's little chapel was a vision of pastoral simplicity,' she writes in *Castles in the Air* – a quote from Hardy perhaps:

> … in its cool, garlanded beauty. I remembered to take a good look around me at the flowers entwined around the gallery balustrade, at the painted angels up on the ceiling and the edifying black-letter text which never failed to move me, 'Watch for you know not ye day or howre'. The bell in the chapel was tolling and the harmonium piped up the Old 100th. Such a sound! To me, so evocative of country churches and clean-shaven young men marching off to war. The door to the chapel was open wide. The drone of the organ floated out and mingled with the pale scent of the fir trees, and the swallows flew in and out, banking hard against the canted ceiling, fanning the cheeks of the angels with their wings.

This was the first proper service since 1921, she says, and she left the chapel in a blizzard of rose petals contrasting with the blizzard that greeted them on their first week in the castle when the sheep had huddled up against the walls to keep alive.

St Beuno, Pistyll (Caernarfonshire)

One of the pilgrim churches for those heading for Bardsey Island, St Beuno (a French saint who also has a cliff-side church dedicated to him at Culbone, Somerset) founded this church in the sixth century. It stands in a walled oval-shaped site that was not only a graveyard but was used as a garden for herbs and rushes which are spread on the floor of the church at Lammastime. The benches and lectern are modern, the tub-shaped font is twelfth century with a Celtic inscription. There was a thatched roof at one time and rope holes can be seen in the roof beams. Outside, the grave of Rupert Davies (1976), the actor who played Maigret, can be found on the east slope (*see colour plate 3*).

MONMOUTHSHIRE

Always a surprise, the church at Llangua is on the Hereford border so we have seen it often. The churches at Bettws Newydd, Kemeys Commander, Llangeview and Llanllywel are all near Usk. Finally, I recommend a walk to see Kilgrrwg on a fine day and, having obtained the key, Mounton is close to the old Severn Bridge so can be combined with a trip to England. (You pay to enter Wales not to leave it).

Bettws Newydd (undedicated)

A couple of miles from the chain bridge over the Usk on the B4598, north of Usk, the village of Bettws Newydd appears to have no church, but it is well hidden up a lane opposite the Alice Springs golf course. It is best to leave a car at the foot of the lane and walk as the entrance to the church is also the entrance to three private houses, one of which is the rectory. It is a small fifteenth-century building standing in a large churchyard with a very old yew tree to the right as you enter the thirteenth-century porch.

Although it has no dedication, Bettws Newydd church was founded by Aeddan, who also built a church at Clytha (ruined) and at Bryngwyn. Is this St Aeddan, a monk who was sent by St David to re-evangalise Ireland and who ended up as Bishop of Ferns where he died in AD 626? If so, Bettws Newydd could dedicate their church to him and celebrate his feast day on 31 January.

However, it is for its screen that this church is most famous. Both rood screen and loft are almost complete. Ridgway and Crossley think very highly of it and only the rood figures of Christ, St John and Mary are missing. The screen has a wooden tympanum, pierced by two three-light windows, and the tympanum has crossed beams so that what is structural also serves as a cross. It would have been wrong to paint this and it is left to the congregation's imagination. However, it is a shame that the interior of the church is not whitewashed as it seems to have been when visited by Ridgway and Crossley in the 1950s. The curved bressumer is carved with grapes, oak leaves and the odd oak apple. The head beam is carved with leaves and under it there are 13 openings almost filled by pointed leaves and grapes on a stem rather like an upside-down wine glass. Unlike St Margaret's in Herefordshire, the screen has no silver sheen but it is only 15ft 5in across (the nave to the font is 20ft) so that it does not appear to be as eye-catching as at Llanano where even the late R.S. Thomas had to concentrate hard to write his poem rather than be overwhelmed by the woodwork.

The two bells in the double bellcote were recast in 1945 in memory of Pilot Officer Berrington and there is a Norman font with cable mounting possibly from an earlier building. The vestry and chimney are a Victorian addition but I have seen worse and they seem to be used for more seating when required.

23 Bettws Newydd church. © Author

24 Screen at Bettws Newydd and rood. © Author

All Saints, Kemeys Commander

Down a small lane leading to a farm, Kemeys Commander (as distinct from Kemeys Inferior) is about 3 miles down the road to Abergavenny from Usk. All Saints church is a grey limestone building much restored by Creed in 1897. Inside (21ft nave) all walls are scraped which makes it very dark. There are two large windows, one very small for the rood loft and one with two lights. The screen has simple perpendicular tracery as at Bettws Newydd where the vicar lives. The bressumer beam is well embedded into the north and south walls, so it looks as if it was built with the church. The church is timber framed and has a barrel roof, seats 28 and is used on two Sundays a month.

Before trying to find Kilgrrwg, it is worth visiting St Jerome, Llangwym Uchaf, south of Usk, which has one of the finest screens in Wales – all complete even if heavily restored by J.P. Seddon in 1896. This church is too large for inclusion here, but is usually open for visitors (see p. 60).

Holy Cross, Kilgrrwg

To reach this little church is a real pilgrimage. Coming from Usk take the road to Newchurch (the 1863 church has an interesting modern window by Theodora Salusbury) and carry on towards Chepstow on a minor road for about 2 miles. At a small crossroads turn left and the hill drops 1:6 alarmingly to a rambling farm at the bottom where you should park and ask the farmer for directions. You need boots as it is a walk over two muddy fields and across a narrow foot bridge then up a steep incline to the walled church surrounded by yew, chestnut, hazel and other trees.

There is a bird screen but the main door was open when we arrived. The grass was neatly cut and inside the whitewashed walls provide the light that is so missed at Kemeys Commander. Founded c.AD 780, this church has a blocked west door, a twelfth-century south door and two fifteenth-century windows. The bell dates from 1696 and the roof was restored in 1989 at a cost of £37,000 (getting the slates to the site must have been a problem). The memorial window (Newbery 1940) is to three men killed in the First World War. Joseph and Fred Bevan were presumably brothers and Richard Morgan, whose military stone is outside, was the last sailor killed in the First World War on HMS *Garland*, a destroyer that had seen action at Jutland.

Outside in the walled churchyard there is an unusual cross that seems to be made from one piece of stone, date unknown. In the Isle of Man this site would be termed a 'Keeil' site, that probably housed a small chapel or site of worship.

Kilgrrwg has an 11.15am service every third Sunday and there are seats for 22 people. The nave is 30ft and there are few more welcoming churches than Holy Cross.

25 St David, Llangeview. © *Author*

St David, Llangeview

This is not only one of the smallest churches in the county, it is also one of the hardest to find. It belongs to the Friends of Friendless Churches and even they recommend buying an OS map (No 152) where it will be found on 397013.

To reach it, take the A449 south from Monmouth, turn off towards Usk on the A472 and at once turn right onto the B4239, then right again after the bridge down a narrow country lane that follows the A449 where, after a mile, there is a grass track leading up to the church. It is best to phone Graig Olway farm first for the key or visit the rectory at Gwernesney. The Friends plan some weekend opening times in September and there is always a service for St David's Day.

Llangeview is spelt Langcyfyw on old documents. St Cyfyw was the son of Gwynlliw Filwr, founder of St Cynyw's church at Llangyniew in Montgomeryshire as well as this one. He was the registrar to his brother Cadog at Llancarfan.

The entrance is at the west end and the relief at getting inside and away from the noisy main road is matched by the silence and the splendour of the non-Victorianised interior. There are nine box pews, a much reduced screen and a square font that is probably Norman. There are two doors in the chancel, one to outside and one to the rood loft, no doubt. The nave is 14ft 4in wide and about 24ft long to the screen. Ridgway and Crossley say that there are still traces of red colouring on some of the mouldings and hollows and that in its heyday it must have been an equal to that at Partrishow.

26 Square font at Llangeview. © *Author*

27 Screen at Llangeview. © *Author*

The squire's box pew was probably under the monument to W. Jones, 1829. The altar rails have twisted balusters. Inside, the whitewashed walls need renewing but the Friends have replaced the barge boards outside and the roof is in good condition. Only the south wall has any windows, plus one in the east wall. There is a large hood-moulded perpendicular three-light window of Bath stone that seems a little out of place as the stone used is old red sandstone, but this is a church of great character, and apart from the large church at Nash near Newport, the only one in the county with a Georgian interior. The pulpit is on the south wall and no one would have been able to sleep in the sermon as the priest would be able to see everything.

Outside there are monuments to many Morgans and Blowers and we were told that the churchyard is so much better looked after now than it was before 1999 when taken over by the Friends.

St James, Llangua

An anomaly, St James is a Church of England church in Wales. Just over the border from Herefordshire into Monmouthshire, it is on the right-hand side of the road down a grassy lane on the main road between Hereford and Abergavenny (A465).

It may have stood on a ford, but the River Monnow floods here and, in Victorian times, the church floor was raised so that the church today is reasonably dry. To get inside, the key can be found at Cap House near the telephone box in the village, or from Powell's Nurseries.

28 St James, Llangua. © *Author*

THE SMALLEST CHURCHES IN WALES

Above: 29 Altar and Candle lighting, Llangua. © *Author*

Right: 30 St James, Llangua. © *Alison Poole*

31 Tombstone at Llangua. © Alison Poole

There is a chancel, nave and Hereford-style wooden square bell tower. The windows are mostly altered from the originals to produce more light. The south nave window is an original. There are wagon roofs in both nave and chancel and a Royal Arms of the late seventeenth century. At the rear of the church is a dark wooden screen from Whitford Chapel in Devon. It has four painted figures, showing Our Lord, the Virgin Mary, King Edward the Martyr and a bishop. They are difficult to see and a powerful torch is required.

On the south wall is a figure of St James with his staff and, originally, a lamp. His boots look so real that any walkers coming here with tired feet might be tempted to do a rapid exchange and no-one would be the wiser. It might make the rest of their walk a lot easier and would certainly impress their friends.

There is seating for only 14 in spite of the 1954 restoration but plenty of space for chairs. At present, Llangua has a service of Holy Communion at 9.30am every third Sunday. One of the visitors here not so long ago was Ellis Peters, creator of the Brother Cadfael stories.

St Llywel, Llanllywel

To find this church, turn right after Llangeview and carry on along the lane for about 3 miles until you see it ahead at a T-junction. It is the same size as Llangeview but lacks its charm.

St Llywell was a companion of St Teilo and went to Dyfed to prevent the king, Aircol Lawhir, from being poisoned. He was granted some land for doing this and has a village in Breconshire dedicated to himself. Breverton considers though that he may well be the same person as St Hywel.

32 St Llywel, Llanllywel. © Author

The key to the church can be obtained from the house opposite if it is locked. There is a stoup in the porch, and a glass jar with holy water, a nice touch not seen anywhere else in Wales. The tympanum over the door is most unusual, with geometrical patterns – Pevsner calls it a flat lintel – perhaps it was graffiti by a wandering mathematician? The top layer has circles, then there are lines with vertical lines underneath. Inside it is rather dark, the screen is modern, the east window restored, with three lights dating from 1300. There is a small Norman window in the west wall between two larger ones that looks strange from the outside.

In one corner are three monuments to members of the Waddington family. One wonders if they are the ancestors of Waddington's board games which were so popular when I was a child.

The church has suffered from slippage over the years and has nasty cracks in one corner. However, it is a must for all travelling mathematicians.

St Andomenus, Mounton

This is a charming little church, well worth two visits, as it is often locked. The vicar at Mathern vicarage has the key. It is down the hill from Chepstow to the roundabout, where you turn left; the car park is behind the church. The one-bay chancel and two-bay nave date from 1860, but were medieval, rebuilt by Walter Evill of Chepstow whose two family windows cheer up the Victorian scene. One shows St Francis with a hare, a robin and other creatures (1962) by Farrar Bell, the other a Virgin, child and St John by Reginald Bell (1933) and on the other wall a 'Sing Out the Lord' by Celtic Studios (1979) with trumpets and string instruments for the Breginton family. All are excellent, especially St Francis.

The altar screen and cross are dedicated to Captain Ian Oswald Liddell VC who died on 21 April 1945, of wounds received after dismantling explosives on the Ems Bridge at Lingen with the 5th Battalion, Coldstream Guards. He went forward by himself onto a defended bridge, clipped the wires and then had to go under the bridge, where he cut wires to two 500lb bombs, then was shot and wounded getting back to his men. He was photographed with his men after they captured the bridge and looks fine in the black and white photograph, but was killed by a sniper seventeen days later.

The church seats 58, is 26ft long and was re-dedicated on 5 April 2005, by Rowan Williams, Archbishop of Canterbury, in a special service. It now has a regular 10.15am service every Sunday.

Mounton is full of old paper mills and the quality of the paper produced here was so good that it was used by the Bank of England for making notes.

PEMBROKESHIRE

Basing ourselves at St Davids, the Chapel of St Non and Our Lady is a short walk from the centre of the town. Meline and Bayvil are close to each other beyond Fishguard. St Govan's Chapel and Caldey St David were visited from Tenby. Llanwnda I had seen in 1974 but it has been tidied up since then and also returning from Fishguard to St Davids we visited St Hywel and St Eloi. Little Newcastle and Llanstinan are close to the A40 and on our way home to Hereford we called at Crinow and then took a diversion to visit little Angle Fishermen's Chapel and ossuary, surely unique not only in Wales but Britain.

Fishermen's Chapel, Angle
A little chapel is behind the church at Angle, appropriately named as the road to it from Pembroke takes more than two right angles to get there. Don't mistake the school for the chapel (the notice in the churchyard points to it) and push very hard to get in the door. We were unable to open the ossuary door, but know it has a barrel ceiling. The main chapel, 9ft x 11ft, has a 1926 Coates Carter (of Caldey Island fame) reredos showing Christ crucified surrounded by working Angle villagers. There is also a male effigy (a bishop perhaps) which might have been moved there from the church. The chapel was built in 1447 by Edward de Shirburn and is dedicated to St Anthony. Edward lived in the fortified old rectory, and the whole place is heavily fortified as it would have made a good landing place for invaders. (see *colour plate 17*).

St Andrew, Bayvil
This is a small Georgian church down a dog-leg lane about 2 miles beyond Nevern towards Moylgrove. It is the hands of the Friends of the Friendless Churches and the key is kept in the house at the end of the lane.

Inside there are box pews, a triple-decker pulpit, a standing bier, slate floor and a late twelfth-century font. In 1980, Roger Clive-Powell restored it. The bellcote has blue slate and the roof looks in reasonable shape but, strangely, there is no sign of any lighting, no candelabra or sign of any oil-lamps.

Presumably the services were all in daylight and, with the door wide open, there is a wonderful view and enough light to read a hymn book.

We visited this church in late summer and found the bier in front of the pulpit as if there had just been a funeral and the coffin had been removed having been blessed on the bier. The clerk would have been busy scribbling at his desk and the clergyman moving from his high desk to the pulpit to say appropriate words about the deceased. I once took a funeral of someone I did not know, but he had lived at West Kirby near Liverpool and as I had been stationed there, it was enough for the relatives just to speak about the place for them to appreciate a few words of sympathy.

33 St Andrew, Bayvil, bier and triple decker pulpit. © *Alison Poole*

St Govan's Chapel, Bosherston

There are places where myth and reality merge in Wales and St Govan's is a good example. A short distance from the village of Bosherston, the road ends in a cliff car park. Sometimes there is a red flag flying as the army use this area for shooting at targets. The cliffs nearby are the home of a family of choughs so the car park is often full of twitchers.

Do not be put off. Take the steps down to the chapel near the south-west side of the car park. Count the steps going down as few people make it the same number coming up. You come to the back of the chapel. Through the open doorway is a square space, 20ft x 12ft, one window looking seawards, a stone bench and altar, carved with a Celtic cross and next to this another door leading into the hermit's tiny cell.

There is a well, covered by a slab, where people used to come for healing with water scooped up in a limpet shell. It was supposed to cure rheumatism, eye diseases and lameness. The west doorway under the bellcote leads towards the sea where there is another well with a reconstructed stone arch.

34 St Govan's Chapel. © *Alison Poole*

35 St David, Caldey Island. © Author

St Govan can be seen on a window in Bosherston church clutching his chapel beneath his beard. In the new Pevsner book on Pembrokeshire, the photographer who took the photo of the chapel must have been confused by the steps as he has it back to front. As hard as I tried, I could not get the number of steps to agree when I went up them with the number coming down. Mystery surrounds the identity of the saint. The most convincing theory is that he was Gobham, abbot of a monastery in Wexford, who crossed the Irish Sea, was pursued by pirates, and put ashore here – some say the rocks opened and swallowed him up – where he lived as a hermit preaching and teaching. He died in 586 and his day is celebrated on 26 March (see *colour plate 19*).

St David, Caldey Island

To get to Caldey Island, you take the boat from Tenby and, if a poor sailor, choose a fine day. The crossing takes about 30 minutes and there is a tractor that takes you to the island, which is star-shaped and measures about 1 mile by 0.5 miles. There is a Cistercian Abbey, with its abbey church, the old church of St Illtyd (all that remains of the old priory), a chocolate factory, two shops, a café that is run from Tenby, and the island church of St David. There are about 40 island inhabitants during the summer.

The building appears to have been square at one stage, then a chancel was added but not in direct line. A final sacristy was then added to the north wall and finally in 1838 the roof, south and east chancel walls were repaired and a porch added that does not appear to have been well joined up to the rest of the church. The main nave is 20ft square with chairs for about 40 and is connected to the chancel by an arch. Rev. Bushell in his guide book states that Flinders Petrie writes about early Irish churches as 'simple quadrangles ... the larger churches present a second oblong of smaller dimensions extending to the east, and constituting the chancel or sanctuary in which the altar is placed, and which is connected with the nave by a triumphal arch or semicircular form.' This is similar to St David, Caldey, but the local limestone has not encouraged the builders to do anything but use very primitive methods, dating from the thirteenth century. Coates Carter, architect of the abbey, restored the building in 1906-7 and again in 1923-5 when he replaced the windows with simple lancets and simple coloured glass by Theodore Baily, one of the local monks.

The font, which is large and looks a bit out of place, is by Eric Gill, 1906, made from Portland stone. In the churchyard all the crosses are made, Celtic cross style, of local oak to a design by Coates Carter as is the preaching cross (1919). There is also a circular tower on the island, probably an observation post, that has a chapel in its upper room which dates from 1907. St David's has regular Sunday services taken by the monks in the Roman Catholic faith.

St Teilo, Crinow (Near Narbeth)
Well worth finding, Crinow is a small hamlet a few miles east of Narbeth. The church stands next to the farm on a sloping churchyard. If locked, the churchwarden lives nearby and kindly arrived in the rain to open the door. The inside of this little church is mostly Victorian, with three three-light windows, 50 seats and monuments all round the walls, including one of 1763 to Richard Mathias. There are three monuments to the Allen family, two brothers killed in the First World War and their father who was in the China Service. There used to be a gallery in this church, probably accessed from outside by steps and a small door, but it was removed and a west window added instead.

The font looks like two pots, one inside the other, but it serves the purpose. This was a church for the big house, Parc Glas, and the squire would look after it, but now, the warden said, it was a struggle to keep it going with a small congregation. The small vestry used to have a boiler with an underfloor pipe for heating and the west end has a metal cap over the end of the pipe. Today there are four electric heaters but the day we visited it was warmer outside than inside. The churchyard, well looked after by the farmer next door, has a nice Celtic cross monument to Blanche Allen by G.E. Halliday (1907) in the north-west corner. Halliday did some work at Llanddewi Velfrey church nearby – the bellcote, pulpit, choirstalls – and may well have been involved with the Crinow restorations.

St Teilo was a local man who studied under Dubricus at Caldey and accompanied David on a trip to Jerusalem. In 547 a plague broke out in Wales and Teilo fled to Brittany, spending seven years at Dol before returning home to Wales.

Right: 1 St Tysilio, Menai Bridge, Anglesey. © *Author*

Below: 2 Holy Cross, Mwnt, Ceredigion. © *Author*

3 St Beuno, Pistyll, Llyn Peninsula. © *Author*

4 St Gredifael, Penmynydd, Anglesey. © *Author*

5 Gronw Tudor and his wife at St Gredifael. © *Author*

Above: 6 St Cwyfan, Llangwyfan. © *Author*

Opposite below: 7 St Mary, Pilleth, Powys. © *B. Lowry*

Right: 8 Holy Well at Pilleth. © *B. Lowry*

Below: 9 Candle lighting at Llanddewi Fach. © *B. Lowry*

10 St Paulinus, Y-Strad-Ffin. © *Author*

11 St David, Rhulen. © *Author*

12 St Issui, Partrishow, Powys. © *Author*

13 Screen at St Anno, Llananno. © *B. Lowry*

14 St Ina, Llanina, Ceredigion. © *Author*

Above: 15 St Catherine, Arthog. © *R.W. Naesmyth of Posso*

Right: 16 Altar at St Teilo, Llandeloy, Pembrokeshire. © *Author*

17 Angle, Fishermen's Chapel. © *Author*

18 St Trillo, Rhos-on-Sea. © *Author*

19 St Govan's Chapel, Pembrokeshire. © *Author*

20 New Hatchment, St Mary the Virgin, Snead. © *Author*

21 St Michaels, Cefnllys, Powys. © *B. Lowry*

22 St Padarn, Llanbadarn-y-Garreg. © *B. Lowry*

23 St Mauritius, Alltmawr. © *B. Lowry*

24 St Ellyw, Llanelieu, Powys. © *B. Lowry*

25 Screen at St Ellyw. © *B. Lowry*

26 St Figel, Llanfigel, Anglesey. © *Author*

27 St Teilo's church at St Fagans Museum. © *Author*

He became famous for rescuing seven small boys from drowning in the River Taf and when he died his body was claimed by Penally, his birthplace, Llandaff, where he had his ministry and Llandeilo Fawr, where he died. The body mysteriously turned into three bodies, thus solving the problem. The skull is in Llandaff Cathedral; it was originally at Llandeilo Llwydarth, near Llangolman (the church having vanished many years ago) and at St Teilo's well nearby, people would come to drink the water from the skull of the saint to cure whooping cough.

St Peter, Little Newcastle

This is a tiny church by the village green which is just to the east of the A40 about halfway between Fishguard and Haverfordwest. It is mostly Victorian, having once had a double nave. Barker pulled down the north nave and added a new chancel with a rather unusual sloping vestry. This has a wooden wall, forming the south side of the chancel, that has a home-made spy-hole, perhaps for the incumbent to see when he should appear.

The glory of this little church is its very modern windows. Most are by Caroline Loveys of the Swansea Institute and were installed in 1996. They depict, on the south side the Crucifixion, Resurrection and Ascension. On the north they show the birth and baptism of Christ. Roy Lewis, head of the Swansea Stained Glass Studio, made the east window in 1962 showing Christ giving the keys of the kingdom to St Peter. In the west end is a 2001 window by John Edwards showing the Second Coming.

36 St Peter, Little Newcastle. © *Author*

There is a twelfth-century font, a memorial to Ann Symons (a relation of the Ann Symons who married Joseph Harries, father of Welsh Newspapers.)

Outside is the monument to Thomas John of Summertown. For details of his involvement with the French Invasion see my *Fishguard Fiasco* (Tenby, 1974). He was a young man with an intense curiosity and was spotted with the French, from whom he purchased two cutlasses for sixpence. He was sent to prison in Haverfordwest, but the French refused to admit that he had committed treason and, as he was a Baptist, it was one Frenchman, Charles Prudhomme (then a prisoner) who said he had been offered 60 guineas to swear against John and another man, Griffith. They were acquitted but John never really recovered from the shock and died at the early age of 38.

Another, more famous, inhabitant of Little Newcastle was the pirate Barti Ddu, whose stone is on the village green. He was born in 1682 and was finally killed by a raid on his ship in the Caribbean by Captain Ogle of the *Swallow* in 1722.

St Eloi, Llandeloy

Not far from Llanhowell, St Eloi's church ceased to be the parish church in 2000 and is now looked after by the Friends of the Friendless Churches. This is a small village with the church tucked away behind the small green on the right of the road as you enter from St David's direction. It is a long, low building divided by a screen. We were unable to find a light switch so had to see it by torchlight but the AMS Transactions No 45 (2001) was at hand and able to give a lot of information.

37 Screen made at Cheltenham, St Eloi, Llandeloy. © *Author*

In Victorian times the church had been used as a school and became a ruin until 1925 when Coates Carter was commissioned to rebuild it. He was helped by a Mrs Thomas, who financed the new wooden screen, made in Cheltenham, in memory of her son Lieutenant Thomas, killed in the First World War. It has a circular stair, which Pevsner says 'allows the minister to appear like a jack-in-the-box'. There is an Arts & Crafts reredos by Carter as at Angle Chapel. The font is probably thirteenth century and there are two square steps up to it.

For details of St Eloi, see St Ellyw of Llanelieu, Powys (p.97). Outside, look among the brambles for the holy well. This church is in need of some regular worshippers and one hopes that it will come back into the parish again when the village expands.

Another Friends church is the Old Parish Church of Manordeifi, near Cardigan close to the River Teifi, so close once that it has its own coracle by the font. It also has several box pews, two with their own fireplaces and some tombs surrounded by fancy carved metal railings. The nave is about 35ft long so I have not included it in this book.

St Hywel, Llanhowel

To find this little church, take the road towards Fishguard from St David's and it is a few miles out down a narrow lane to the right marked with the Church Trail signs. The raised churchyard was taken over by moles and a noisy rookery when we called but inside all was peace and quiet.

38 St Hywel, Llanhowel. © *Author*

The building was restored in 1888 and re-roofed by E.V. Collier in 1909. Inside it is whitewashed with new, very comfortable pews and a warm carpet. The corbels remain of a rood screen and in the west wall is a blocked-up leper's squint. All is light and bright and the large stone at the back, which says 'Rinacus and Martyr' seems out of place.

St Hywel, a friend of St Teilo, fled to Brittany, where he was famous as a warrior and for his chivalry in coming to the aid of King Arthur in Britain. He is mentioned by Geoffrey of Monmouth and by The Mabinogian. St Hywel is pictured in M. Hawkett's panel in the cross passage between chancel and north chapel which commemorates two members of the Pringle family killed in the First and Second World Wars. The other war memorial on the north wall commemorates three seafarers killed in the First World War, a fisherman, a merchant seaman and a naval seaman. Under their names are the words: 'in gratitude for safe return of others'.

St Justinian, Llanstinan

This must be one of the remotest churches in Pembrokeshire that is still open for services. To find it, take the A40 north from Haverfordwest and halfway you pass the Pant y Phillip estate and a short distance further there is an entrance to a quarry with the sign for St Justinian's church. The road is very bumpy and only suitable for 4-wheel-drive vehicles but it is only a 10 minute walk to the newly enlarged house, where you keep right, cross over the little bridge and the church is over the field of sheep ahead. The churchyard seems Celtic in origin, circular and full of brambles and broken tombs. The church is in good condition though and the chancel is newly reslated. The windows are painted green and are sash, like a house; the whitewashed walls have only one wall monument, to the Rev. Henry Miles and his wife. He was rector for 38 years at the turn of the century. The other monument by the altar is to Fanny Owens who died in 1835 aged two months. She was the daughter of Sir John Owens who purchased Llanstinan House from the Knox family. It was Thomas Knox who commanded the Fishguard Fencibles in 1797 and, after firing one shot, retreated from Fishguard in 1797 when the French landed nearby.

There is a bat box outside and an exterior bell rope as at St Hywel's church. Also, like that church, St Justinian's has a diagonal passage connecting the side chapel with the nave and serving as a squint so congregation members could see the altar.

St Justinian was David's confessor and lived in a cell on Ramsey Island, having banished all women from the island. He was very strict with his followers, who revolted and cut off his head in 537, and where it fell a spring of water spilled out of the earth. He is supposed to have snatched up his head, crossed the sound and collapsed where his chapel was built. His murderers became lepers and were forced to live on the little rock between Ramsey and the mainland known as Leper's Rock. The church is looked after by Rev. Barnes from Goodwick who has a regular service.

39 St Justinian, Llanstinan. © *Author*

40 St Justinian, altar. © *Author*

41 St Gwyndaf, Llanwnda. © *Alison Poole*

St Gwyndaf, Llanwnda

Perched up on the hill above Goodwick Sands, Llanwnda is a recently restored, simple church with double belfry and is full of character. For a start, you can walk round the building searching for the six stone crosses which date from the seventh to the ninth century. The best, by the east of the south transept, is a face that looks as if it is done up in a scarf under a rough cross of St Andrew. Is she a nun perhaps?

There is a squint in the porch, perhaps for lepers to look inside to see the host at Eucharist. The ancient roof with king posts dates from the fifteenth century and one has a carving of a monk.

The two bells are post-war and dedicated to the Fishguard ferries, *St David* and *St Patrick* – which were sunk during the war – and to their crews.

Outside the church, it is a short walk to Carregwastad Point. Here, on 22 February 1797, Colonel Tate, an Irish American, landed with a thousand men of the Black Legion. They were wet, cold and very hungry as many had been in chains as political prisoners. They entered the church, lit a fire using paper from the parish register, pinched the church plate (later recovered from a pawn shop in Carmarthen) and marched off to Trehowel Farm which became Tate's headquarters. Three days later he surrendered to a mixed force of sailors, fencibles and militia. Tradition has it that Cawdor persuaded the ladies of Fishguard to stand on rocks in their stove-pipe hats and red shawls so they looked like guardsmen from a distance. However, the French were too hungry and too drunk on Portuguese wine from Trehowel to fight and most of them were happy to go into captivity. Nearby Garn Fawr hillfort was used by the French as a lookout post.

Gwyndaf, depicted in a long cloak sitting on a pony in Goodwick school's badge, was a Breton and friend of St Aidan. They quarrelled over the naming of a well; Gwyndaf lost and cursed the stream so it no longer carried fish. He made up for it by founding Llanwnda and his own well nearby. When he died, his body was taken to be buried with other saints on Bardsey Island.

St Dogfael, Meline

This church is close to Bayvil off the A487 Fishguard to Cardigan road. It stands down a lane on a raised site so, though Pevsner calls it 'An object lesson in High Victorian solid geometry' and tells you it was built by R.J. Withers, for Sir Thomas Lloyd of Bronwydd, this was a much older church originally. Alas, all the medieval parts have vanished with the sole exception of a delightful filled-in west door with amazing label-stops with carved faces. Is this in situ or is it from some other building?

42 St Dogfael, Meline, label-stops. © *Alison Poole*

43 St Dogfael, Meline. © Alison Poole

Inside, the church has an octagonal font and a rose west window supposed to have come from Bronwydd House. All is simple and High Victorian, but the reredos of stone has some very fine coloured tiles of five colours which go well with the stained glass by Lavers and Barraud in the east window.

If you are still puzzled as to how to get into this church, then remember that most church keys are too large for the pocket or to go for duplication and you will find it nearby.

Chapel of St Non and Our Lady, St Davids

An easy walk from the centre of St Davids (turn left at the end of the main street, not right for Fishguard) but worth doing on a fine day as there is no shelter. St Non or Nonna was the mother of St David and came from a noble family. She has a church in Alternum, Cornwall, dedicated to her and her tomb is at Dirinon in Brittany. The ruins of the chapel are in a field with two small standing stones. There is a Roman Catholic retreat house and a chapel built in the 1930s by David Thomas. It has glass from the Morris Studios, measuring 25ft x 12ft, but appears unused today. The altar is made from a collection of odds and ends – a stone with a square hole etc. – and when we went to see it, the roof contained a swallow's nest so the Retreat House Warden kept the door open for the birds to fly in and out.

44 Chapel of Our Lady and St Non, St Davids. © *Author*

WILDLIFE IN CHURCHYARDS

William Condry in *The Natural History of Wales* (Collins New Naturalist, No 66) writes of rare plants found in churchyards, including:

Guilsfield, Powys	Dusky Crane's Bill
Carno, Ceredigion	Melancholy Thistle
Clyro, Powys	Cyclamen
Llanbadarn, Aberystwyth	Large Quaking Grass
Penegoes, St Cadfarch	Keeled Garlic
(Has a memorial to Richard Wilson, RA d.1732)	
Haverfordwest, St Ishmael	Bear's Breech, Star of Bethlehem
Penalt, Monmouthshire	Goldilocks buttercup
Tregaron, Ceredigion	Danish scurvygrass

Lichens on church walls and gravestones need respect and of course bird nests – like the swallow's nest inside the RC chapel in St Non's Bay – must not be disturbed even if it means leaving the door open. More details can be obtained from Caring for God's Acre, 6 West St Leominster, Herefordshire.

POWYS

The threefold counties that make up Powys were mostly visited on day trips from Hereford. Thus Alltmawr (worth finding), Bettws Chapel (near Hay), Cascob, Cefnllys, Colva, Cregrina Pilleth and Rhulen were seen from Hereford. We stayed in Meifod to visit the Quaker Meeting House, Dolobran and Pennant Melangell. Partrishow and Capel-y-Ffin are best seen from Abergavenny. I do not recommend the road from Hay. Little Llanbadarn-y-Garreg is near Cregrina but we went on a wet day and needed boots. Snead is on the border and can be seen leaving the A49 at Craven Arms. Llananno we just managed to stop at and found enchanting. St Ellyw was seen on the same day as Alltmawr and was a surprise. We must have called on a Potters' Convention as there were no people, cars in plenty and the church looked as if it had not been visited for weeks. Llanddewi Fach is near Painscastle.

St Mauritius, Alltmawr (Breconshire)

This is one of the smallest church in Wales and can be found just off the main road between Builth Wells and Talgarth (A470) on the west side going towards Builth; about 4 miles short of that town is a steep left-hand bend with no sign. Up here to the right is a narrow footpath that leads to this little building which may be seventeenth century but was given a three-sided apse in the nineteenth century.

45 St Mauritius, Alltmawr. © B. Lowry

Mauritius is the Dutch for Maurice. The island in the Atlantic was originally called Cerné, a Portuguese name, but the Dutch in 1598 called it after their stadholder Maurice of Nassau. Why is the fifth smallest church in Wales called after Maurice? He was a Christian soldier of the Theban Legion. He refused to take part in a massacre of Christians when ordered by the Emperor Maximinian (AD 287) who ordered his soldiers to turn on Maurice and his legion and upwards of 6000 men were put to the sword. His feast day is 22 September.

Inside, this little church is a delight. It measures 27ft from font to altar step. There are three box pews – for the local squire and his family, no doubt – and 12 ordinary pews. The three oil lamps have been converted to electricity and there is a three-sided apse. There are two monuments, one dated 1822 and one of the 1930s to Alfred Tristran Lawrence, Baron Trevethen of Blaengawney who was drowned in the River Wye when fishing in 1936. He was 93. His wife is shown with him in relief – she died in her fifties in 1931. The Baron was Lord Chief Justice of England between 1921 and 1922 but one suspects that fishing was his first love and when we came away from this church on an April afternoon, there was a man fishing below on the banks of the Wye – perhaps the Baron's ghost?

Holy Trinity, Bettws (Radnorshire)

To find this little chapel of ease to Clyro, take the Brecon road from Hereford and just before the turning over the Wye to Hay you find the half-timbered Rhydspence Inn on the border between Radnorshire and Hereford.

46 Holy Trinity, Bettws. © *Author*

47 Screen and altar at Holy Trinity. © *Author*

Take the windy hill behind the inn past several houses until a T-junction where you turn left and left again at the track to Chapel Farm. Opposite is a bungalow, Aylton Lea, where the large key to the chapel is kept. Continue about 100yds towards the farm, park, and go through the gate over the field on your left to the Victorian chapel. There is also a key at Nash Dom nearby.

In fact, the building has a fourteenth-century roof, a single bell and a thirteenth-century font borrowed from Clyro church. The rest is the work of F.R. Kempson of Hereford who spent £400 restoring it in 1878. Here the young curate, Rev. Francis Kilvert, walked from Clyro on St Valentine's Eve, 1870: ' … wrapped in two waistcoats, two coats, a muffler and a mackintosh and was not at all too warm. Hear the chapel bell pealing … and, when I got to the chapel, my beard, moustache and whiskers were so stiff I could hardly open my mouth and my beard was frozen onto my mackintosh. There was a large christening party from Llwyn Gwilym. The baby was baptized in ice which was broken and swimming about in the font.'

KILVERT

The Rev. Francis Kilvert was born in the rectory, Hardenhuish, near Chippenham in 1840, the son of the rector. He was educated privately and at Wadham College, Oxford, later becoming curate to his father. In 1865, he moved to Clyro near Hay and spent seven happy years. Five years later he started his diary which runs for nine years until his early death from peritonitis. It was first published by his nephew in 1938 and has been compared with Pepys. I have used the Cape 1944 edition, edited by William Plomer. For details of the Kilvert Society, write to the Hon. Secretary, Lawrence Jackson at 10a Manor Road, Sherborne St John, Basingstoke, Hants RG24 9JL

One hundred and thirty six years later I made the journey (by car, but by foot across the field) but the weather was bright and cold with lambs skipping about in the farm below. One wonders if the baby went on to become an Antarctic explorer? In August 1872 Kilvert took his last journey to the 'dear old chapel' and preached a farewell sermon from I Philippians, 3: 'I thank my God upon every remembrance of you'. Later he burst into tears. His diary records 'a sad, sad day'.

48 Holy Trinity, Beltws from the east. © Alison Poole

Capel-y-Ffin, St Mary (Breconshire)

The little church at Capel-y-Ffin can be found on the minor road that runs off the A465 to Llanthony Priory. The building, 'owl-like', as the Victorian diarist Kilvert describes it, stands by the Honddu stream where there is a narrow bridge. The wooden bell turret leans dramatically inwards but inside you are in a Georgian chapel, 25ft x 13ft, dating from 1764 with seating downstairs, on benches with backs, for about 20 and room for a further 20 (small ones) upstairs where there is a bench running the length of the north wall. On the east window are the words from Psalm 121, 'I will lift up mine eyes unto the hills from whence cometh my help' dating from 1991 when the window was restored in memory of Sir Alec Morrison. The pulpit (which has recently lost its floor) dates from 1780 and the font is medieval with a broken rim. The graveyard has seven ancient yews and there must have been an earlier building, although there is a small Baptist Chapel on the other side of the Honddu.

Eric Gill, the typographer, came to live here late in 1924 with David Jones, the artist and poet. They took over the monastery building (now a private house) and although they had their own chapel there, they no doubt attended Capel-y-Ffin where there are two tombstones that may well be made by Gill or one of his colleagues. One is to Charles Stones, Carpenter, died 1935, who helped Gill as a handyman.

The name Capel-y-Ffin means 'Chapel of the Boundary' as it stands on the boundary of three counties – Herefordshire, Monmouthshire and Breconshire. It also stands of the boundary of three dioceses: Hereford, St David's and Llandaff. On leaving the church, the brave motorist can take the gospel pass north to Hay-on-Wye but it is not recommended for large cars as the passing places are small in the extreme. There is a pony-trekking centre at Llanthony as well as an inn and the Abbey Hotel.

St Michael, Cascob (Radnorshire)

In Domesday Book, Cascob was 'Cascope', mound over the River Cas. Today the mound is still there in a large circular churchyard with a very old yew tree. It has the tower and belfry on it, which seems to have an older base. Was it once a defensive tower? The passage inside from the west wall through to the bell tower is almost 6ft thick with a strange pointed door and one can see right up to the top of the tower.

Only one bell is used today and the stairs up to the bell chamber are not safe for visitors.

49 St Mary, Capel-y-Ffin.
© *Author*

50 St Michael and sheep. © *B. Lowry*

THE SMALLEST CHURCHES IN WALES

51 St Michael, roof and screen. © *B. Lowry*

ABRACADABRA
charm found in Cascob church

ABRACADABRA
ABRACADABR
ABRACADAB
ABRACADA
ABRACAD
ABRACA
ABRA
ABR
AB
A

In the name of the Father, Sun & of the Holy Ghost Amen xxx and in the name of the Lord Jesus Christ I will relive (relieve) Elizabeth Loyd from all witchcraft and from all Evil spirites & from all evil men or Women or Wizardes or hardness of hart Amen x x x (then follows doggerel Latin)
And into that universal nature God will interpose [himself?] against skill diabolical Amen xxx [Psa: XLIV] He raised up my heart, I indite a good matter touching the King. O Lord open Thou my lips & my tongue shall shew forth Thy praise, to turn aside the grasp of the wicked and malignant. Lord Jesus Christ Saviour of mankind I bereach [beseech] the preserver of Elizabeth Loodyd from all witchcraft evil men or women & from all spirites or wizards or hardnes of hart Amen x x x & this I will trust in the Lord Jesus Christ my Readeemer and Saviour from all witchcraft and from all other men or women and from all assaltes of evil spirites of men or devils & this I will trust in the Lord Jesus Christ my Redeemer & Saviour from all Evil Spirites & from all other assaltes of the Devil and that he will Relive [relieve] Elizabeth Loyd from all witchcraft and from all evil spirites by the same apower as he deid cause the blind to see, the lame to walke, & the dum to talke & that thou findest with unclean spirits to be in thire one mindes Amen … as weeth [willeth?] Jehovah Amen. The witches compassed her abought but in the name of the Lord I will destroy them Amen x x x x x x

Pater pater pater Noster, Noster, Noster ave ave ave Maria Creed ro paclorn [in saecula saeculorum ?] x on x adonay x Tetragammaton [Jehovah] x Amen & in the name of the Holy Trinity & of Hubert preserved the above mind and body from all Desesis & from all witchcraft and from all other assaltes of the Devil, Amen. O Lord Jesus Christ we beseeth thee for thy mercy grant that this holy charm ABRACADABRA may cure they servant Elizabeth Loyd from all Evil Spirites and from all ther desesis Amen x x x
By Jah Jah Jah

The key to the church is obtained from the cottage near the gate and the latter must be kept shut or the sheep might escape. Inside, the south wall is curved and the screen dates from the fourteenth century, a simple construction with the parapet of the rood loft still in place and five round-headed lights each side of the doorway.

In the chancel is a monument to Welsh Scholar W. Jenkins Rees (1806-55) who was the author of Canbro British Saints and did much to restore the Eisteddford. Nearer the tower is the 'Abracadabra charm'; dating from the seventeenth century it was used to exorcise demons from Elizabeth Lloyd. Mary Webb's novel *Precious Bane* has much on witchcraft and was written about Shropshire, and Leominster Priory has a (useable) ducking stool in the nave so witchcraft in the seventeenth and eighteenth centuries was not far away. There is a handsome beech tree in the churchyard planted for the coronation of King George VI in 1937.

St Michael, Cefnllys (Radnorshire)

Just to the west of Llandrindod Wells and on the River Ithon, Cefnllys has a large iron-age hillfort with the ruins of a Mortimer thirteenth-century castle on the top. Later, a house was built on the site by the last castle constable and this was recorded as a ruin by Camden in 1558.

The church can be reached by a footbridge from the picnic site, over the river and round a field. The church is lucky to have a Jacobean pulpit and a six-light east and six-light north screen with a tiled floor. The Rev. Davies in his book *The Ancient Celtic Church of Wales* relates how in 1893 the Rector of Llandrindod,

52 St Michael, Cefnllys; Castle Hill behind. © *B. Lowry*

53 St Michael before destruction. © *Rev. D. Davies*

54 St Michael, after 1893 de-roofing. © *Rev. D. Davies*

who had a large rectory next to his new town church wanted to fill it with a decent congregation. He also preferred to have services in English so, at his own responsibility, he deliberately unroofed St Michael's and the old church of Llandrindod (which was single chamber, thirteenth or fourteenth century with box pews) so that, he thought, the Welsh would flock to his inner town church. After two years the Bishop commissioned Nicholson & Son, architects, to re-roof both churches and both were resurrected. Much was lost, including the entire character of the Holy Trinity, Llandrindod, but Davies obtained drawings of them and his picture of the early Cefnllys and its ruin are shown here *(see colour plate 20)*.

St David, Colva (Radnorshire)

To reach Colva, one of the highest churches in Wales, take the A44 to Rhayader, turning off at Old Radnor (worth a visit for its long Gloucester-made screen) to Hengoed where a minor road climbs to Colva. The church stands at the end of the village at the side of a hill. St David is basically thirteenth century with a typical timbered fifteenth-century Radnorshire porch. The inside is basic, with some hard-to-read biblical inscriptions and a memento mori (skull and crossbones) by the AD 1200 circular font. At the west end is a large Royal Arms of George II, adapted for Queen Victoria. It has the name of the maker – Cartwright of Aberedow on the base along with Thos. Davies, churchwarden. The boarded-off

55 St David, Colva. © *B. Lowry* (see also front cover)

56 St David, pulpit and altar. © *B. Lowry*

57 Memento mori at Colva. © *B. Lowry*

58 Coat of arms, Colva. © B. Lowry

west end houses the two bells above. One has 1707 and the names 'Edward Powell and John Minton' and the other, of 1740, has 'Come away without delay'. There is a coffin table at the west end.

Here came Kilvert with a boy on foot from Clyro in February, 1870. He stopped at the Sun Inn (now the farm next to the church) and consumed 'a pint of excellent light brown beer, some hard sweet home-baked bread, and some hard cheese.' He then tried the Colva 'echo' 'In the field next the belfry and west end of the poor, humble, dear little whitewashed church.' He said it was 'very clear, sharp and perfect.'

The seats appear to have come from a local school and the little organ is in a gap between them. The slates were replaced by wooden shingles in 1981-2 but more work needs to be done to save this little church from becoming ruinous. It is no longer whitewashed and on a very cold day Colva is not a place to spend much time outside.

St David, Cregrina (Radnorshire)

This is a whitewashed church standing high above a bridge over the River Edw, not far from Colva. The churchyard is large and circular, like Cascob, but the porchless church is very different. Like Llangar, it is constructed in two pieces and they do not line up with each other. The nave, restored in 1903, is joined by a simple screen positioned at an angle of about 15° sloping to the right facing the altar. The roof is also slightly different. The pegs have been left in the nave timbers but the wind-braces, arched beams and tie beams of the chancel are neater and it seems almost that if the screen had been replaced by a wall there would be two different churches. Each has its own door.

60 St David, screen and roof. © *B. Lowry*

Opposite: 59 St David, Cregrina. © *B. Lowry*

There are two services a month here and the list of rectors shows the first was Rev. J. Hergest in 1685 and the last one on the board is Rev. P.A. Pearcey in 1979. Cregrina is an enchanting church and worth going out of one's way to discover.

Friends' Meeting House, Dolobran, near Meifod (Montgomeryshire)

This is well worth discovering and needs a good map as to reach it you take a hilly footpath over two fields from the Pontrobert Road.

It is a brick built, 1700 building with a cottage on the left and a meeting house on the right. The door to the meeting house was larger but has been reduced in size. The windows have attractive drip courses over them and there are copings on the gables with a wooden gallery staircase at the rear, seldom used. An outside WC completes the scene. Haslam states that all the furnishings were taken to 'Pennsylvania and elsewhere' when the Friends moved out in 1870. Now they are back and the sliding wall between the cottage and the meeting house has been filled in – but could be restored if required. The meeting house, 20ft x 22ft, has the usual backed benches with central small table with a real atmosphere of peace and quiet. Much of the restoration was by the Lloyd family, iron founders, and two of the stones by the gate are in fact made of iron from the Lloyd foundry.

61 Dolobran Meeting House. © *Author*

62 Inside Dolobran, July 2006. © *Author*

St Anno, Llananno (Radnorshire)

Easily found, this church is tucked into the side of the A483 a few miles north of Llandrindod Wells. This is where one day the poet R.S. Thomas came and wrote his poem complaining about the traffic speeding past, noticing the reflection of the church in the River Ithon:

> There are few services
> now; the screen has nothing
> to hide. Face to face
> with no intermediary
> between me and God, and only the water's
> quiet insistence on a time
> older than man, I keep my eyes
> open and am not dazzled …

The church is famous for its screen and rood loft, which date from the late fifteenth century. The makers were the Newtown School who designed a screen in Newtown – no longer present – and in Llanwnog church in Montgomeryshire. However, Llananno's screen is probably the finest in Wales. The two bressumers are carved with pomegranates with vine leaves coming from the mouths of what look like serpents, but what Haslam calls 'wyverns'. On the parapet are 25 figures (replacements carved in 1880 by Boulton of Cheltenham) representing, on the left the kings, prophets and patriarchs and with Christ in the centre, the 12 apostles to the right.

The altar front is simpler, of course, and the three-light east window with one central coloured addition is arranged to give maximum light into what is rather a dark little church. There is one remaining box pew marked 'David Lewis, Warden, 1681' and the church registers go back to 1781.

Outside by the river and a neatly laid hedge is the modern grave of the landlord of the Red Lion with a neat picture of his pub on the stone.

The architect, Walker of Liverpool, who preserved the screen, deserves our thanks. It is worth exploring and, when inside, the noise of the traffic is not heard so one can sit with one's eyes open and enjoy the peace and the screen that has nothing to hide (see *colour plate 13*).

St Padarn, Llanbadarn-y-Garreg (Radnorshire)

This square little church, the smallest in Radnorshire, is further down the valley from Cregina and stands, whitewashed, by a stream. Inside it has a simple scissor-truss roof, a very faded Royal Arms, seventeenth-century altar rails and pulpit and eighteenth-century windows. Restored in 1960, it is in need of some more attention today.

St Padarn, abbot, bishop and confessor, was the son of Petran and Guean and came from a noble race. His father was always off on campaigns and his mother Guean looked after the boy. One day she put a cloth that the baby had been wrapped in to dry in their castle window. It was promptly taken by an eagle, a sign the boy was due for greatness, and a year later the cloth that had lined the eagle's nest was recovered intact. When he was a young man, he set off to find his father, discovering him in Ireland but unable to get him to come home; St Padarn became a monk and founded a monastery at Mauritana. He made enemies with Maelgwyn, a local chief, who left him three hampers to look after, returning later and accusing Padarn and two others of stealing from them. In fact, the hampers had been filled with moss and stones so it was a trick. All three had their hands immersed in boiling water and two suffered, but not Padarn. Later, Maelgwyn became blind, was cured by Padarn and given land in Rheidol. He was then an abbot and went with Teilo and David to visit Jerusalem. Padarn was presented with a cope, which one of his monks, Arthur, tried to steal. Arthur was buried in earth up to his neck in punishment. After 21 years in Wales – living in Powys – he returned to his mother's home in Letavia (?Latvia) where he died. According to his biographer his body was brought back to be buried at Llanbadarn, but whether Llanbadarn Fawr, Llanbadarn Fynydd or the little riverside church at Llanbadarn-y-Garreg, I do not know.

63 St Padarn, Llanbadarn-y-Garreg altar and faded coat of arms. © *B. Lowry*

64 St David, Llanddewi Fach, from the field. © B. Lowry

St David, Llanddewi Fach (Radnorshire)

To find this church you must take a narrow winding lane signposted Llanddewi Fach church from Painscastle. After considerable ups and downs, the lane ends at a farm. Leave your vehicle here and take the footpath from the top edge of the farmhouse. This runs across a field which was full of recently cut-down nettles when we visited it. The church stands on an old site and dates from 1860, when rebuilt by Seddon and Prichard. The porch suffers from bad cracks and it seems the building is gradually slipping downhill.

Inside, the Victorian pews have added candle holders at each end and there are four oil lamps used for services, held twice a month at the moment. There was a small wine bottle for the eucharist on one of the pews. Presumably, one wears heavy clothes in winter as the Victorian fireplace showed no signs of use. There are seats for about twenty-four, two bells and two seventeenth-century benches. There is a chalice of 1624 inscribed 'his is the common cupp of the Parishe of Glandue Vach' and the porch floor has been constructed from the grave of Lewis Griffiths who died in 1691. Francis Kilvert writes in October 1878, that he came with a choir to Clyro and sang at Painscastle, Glasbury and Llanddewi: ' … an excellent hearty choral service. In the evening Tom Williams gave a supper to his choir and their helpers and we passed a pleasant musical evening. To my surprise I sang three songs.'

The 'church in the fields' has an atmosphere all its own, an essential stillness, and when we called, a buzzard in the yew tree seemed to be its solitary guardian.

65 St David, Llanddewi Fach. © *B. Lowry*

66 St Ellyw, Llanelieu. © *B. Lowry*

St Ellyw, Llanelieu (Breconshire)

Llanelieu is a tiny hamlet with a pottery about 2 miles south of Talgarth. Follow the signs to the pottery from Talgarth, past St Gwendoline's church and up a hill which eventually arrives at Llanelieu. The church stands in a field – in fact the churchyard is rather overgrown – and there is a small car park above it. The large key can be collected from the glass-fronted house opposite the pottery.

Strangely, there were lots of cars but no people when we called and no sign of anyone using the church which belongs to the Friends of Friendless Churches. There is a priest's door, thirteenth century, and another door, blocked, to the right of the main porch. Baldwin of Brecon made some repairs in 1905 and probably removed the old door and opened up a new doorway, adding the porch bellcote and a new roof. The screen is most unusual, fourteenth century, with a veranda of posts supporting once a floor and no doubt a ladder for players, against a purple-red coloured screen with white roses and a white cross which must have looked very fine when created. There are several monuments to the Aubreys and one to Walter Watkins, d.1773, who left 10 shillings to help 'two children lawfully begot yearly and for ever'. There are pews for 20, a north wall royal coat of arms and outside a couple of pillar stones by the porch which may date to the seventh century, as well as a sundial of 1686.

Who was St Ellyw? The Dictionary of Saints does not mention him but does mention St Eloi, Bishop of Noyon, who was not only a talented goldsmith but also tried his hand at becoming a blacksmith. He found this more difficult because the horse would not keep still. However, he solved this problem by cutting off the leg he was working on, replacing the horseshoe and then restoring the leg to the horse which apparently survived. He is also shown in Angers Cathedral as leading the devil by holding his nose by a pair of blacksmith's pincers. He would have been a useful, practical person to have at Llanelieu where the Friends have much work to do to keep this little church going.

It has been researched in 'Carmarthenshire Snippets' that St Ellyw was in fact not the same person as St Eloi, who was a disciple of St Cadog of Llancarfan. Breverton says Ellyw was a grand-daughter of Brychan.

St Issui, Partrishow (Breconshire)

St Issui, a holy man, had a cell near here with a sacred well. To find Partrishow (or Patricio in Welsh) take the road to Llanthony (off the A465 near Abergavenny) and after a few miles there is a road to the left that gets very narrow and climbs up a valley between trees.

Suddenly you come to the lychgate erected in 1908 by the late Richard Baker Gabb, who was largely responsible for restoring the church, work he put in the hands of W.D. Caröe. There is a chapel to St Issui with his tomb and altar above. This has a grille looking into the main church, which Haslam considers is older.

67 St Issui, Partrishow in springtime. © Author

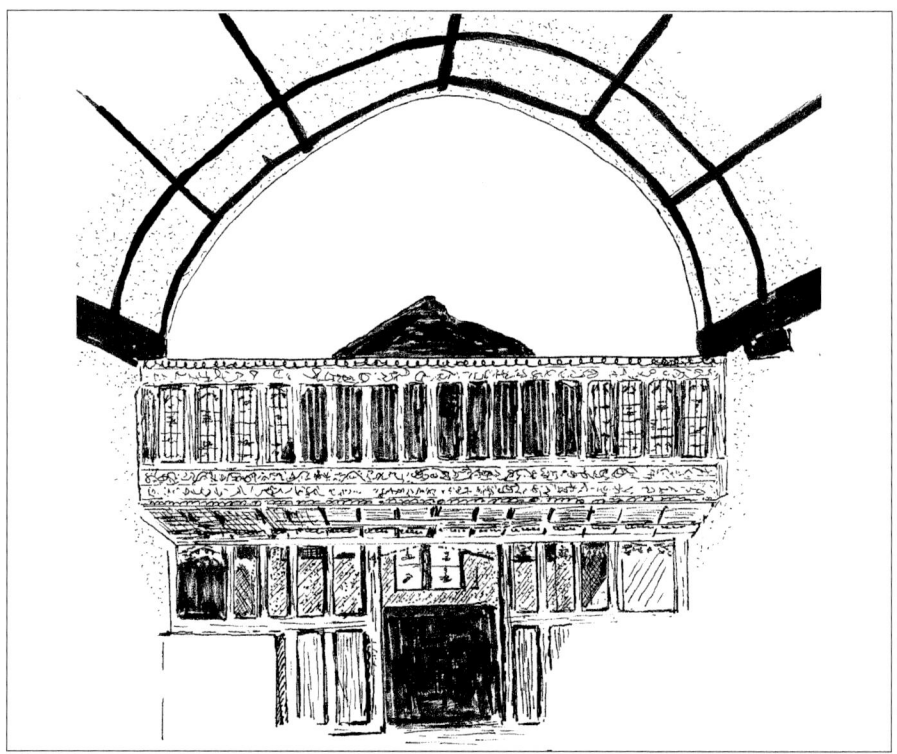

68 Rood Screen, Partrishow. © Alison Poole

It is a Norman building with Tudor south windows and Elizabethan perpendicular chancel. The screen and rood loft, which date from 1500, rival that at St Margaret's,* and it retains its stair so that it ties in well with the barrel ceiling of the nave.

There are wall paintings including a Doom Figure, who looks as if he has a miner's lamp, Royal Arms, and a font believed to date from 1055. Amongst the memorials to Powells and Griffiths is a small one to a seventeen-year-old girl from Peebles, Patricia Wolfe-Murray, whose grandfather was the vicar here before the last war.

Outside there is a stone bench along the base of the wall by the porch – probably build to strengthen the wall as well as to give weary travellers a grand view. There is also a lean-to stable building for the vicar's horse. There is a Eucharist service here on the first and third Sundays of the month. Partrishow is a church worth going miles to see. It has a real atmosphere about it and needs much support.

St Melangell, Pennant Melangell (Montgomeryshire)

People go on pilgrimages to the Holy Land, to Lourdes and to Compostella for spiritual refreshment, peace of mind and body or simply because they think that they will be given time to think on the journey and that the journey is almost more important than the arrival. Nowhere is this more appropriate than going to the shrine of St Melangell. To get there, take the road to Llangynog and then wind your way down a minor lane in the Tanat Valley.

The feast day of St Melangell falls on 27 May. She was an Irish chieftain's daughter who fled to Wales as her father had arranged for her to marry someone she disliked. She settled in Pennant in the Berwyn Hills where she made friends with the wild animals, especially hares. When a local chief, Brochwel, came out hunting hares, he found his hounds were frightened to chase one hare which was hiding under the dress of Melangell who was kneeling in prayer. When he raises his horn to his lips, it sticks there. When she sees him, he realises that she is a holy person, gives her land and encourages her to form a religious community which still exists today. All hares in the valley are free from hunting and St Melangell is the patron saint of hares.

The church is basically mid-twelfth century with nave, long chancel, offertory (with the shrine of St Melangell) and the apse with St Melangell's tomb on the south side and known as the cell y bedd. The vestry has a bookshop which seems to be unmanned but no doubt it has helpers when there are crowds of visitors. The restoration work began in 1988 and finished in 1992 at a total cost of £170,000 which is cheap by today's standards as it included the rebuilding of the shrine. The only other shrine of this kind in the country is at Westminster Abbey (King Edward the Confessor) so there was considerable research to be done. The architect, R.B. Heaton, is to be congratulated.

---

* See *Discovering the Smallest Churches in England*, p. 61.

69 St Melangell, Pennant Melangell. © Author

The church is open throughout the year. There is a 3.00pm Sunday evensong, an 8.30am morning prayer during the week as well as midday prayer and a 6.00pm evensong. For details of special services contact The Church Office, Pennant Melangell, Llangynog WY10 0HQ. The churchyard has some very ancient yews and a beautiful stone carving of a hare symbol and the words 'Pererindod Melangell'.

St Mary, Pilleth (Radnorshire)
Slightly larger than most of my churches, Pilleth is a remarkable church for several reasons. Firstly, it stands on the site of a famous battle between Owen Glendower and the Earl of Mortimer in 1402. Mortimer was defeated by Glendower's ambush, but he was well treated by the Welsh leader, eventually marrying his daughter. In 1870, the Price family found bones on the hillside and they planted a rectangular plantation of fir trees in memory of the fallen.

The battle is mentioned in Shakespeare's *Henry IV, Part I*:

> The noble Mortimer
> Leading the men of Herefordshire to fight
> Against the wild and irregular Glendower
> Was by the rude hand of that Welshman taken
> A thousand of his people butchered.

70 St Mary, Pilleth. © *B. Lowry*

There is an unmarked gravel track up to the church and some rather unnecessary stone steps to the churchyard, where there is a magnificent view over the Lugg Valley. In the 1960s, when I first came here, the church had not been whitewashed and there was a Civil War sword and breastplate in the church. Now the roof has been rebuilt and the inside is whitewashed as well. There are organised quiet days and a Friends of St Mary group to prevent the building from being forgotten.

The church consists of a long nave and tower of early fourteenth-century date. There was a south-west tower stair-turret, as by the holy well (full of frogs) is a masonry pile that looks as if part of the tower fell at some period. In 1894 a fire destroyed the roof and it was restored by W.J. Tapper in 1911. This roof has been rebuilt by the Hereford firm of Hook Mason.

There is a magnificent font, a flat ogee-headed piscina, about 100 chairs and a lobed stoup. One of the windows looks as if it was falling out but outside a new buttress prevents this.

The Friends of Pilleth had 16 services and events planned for 2007, including 3pm prayer book evensongs, four Celtic eucharists, three quiet days and a confirmation service to be conducted by the Bishop of Swansea and Brecon. For further details, contact Peter Hood, churchwarden (01547 560272).

71 St David, Rhulen – altar with flowers. © B. Lowry

Rhulen, St David (Radnorshire)

This little church, recently whitewashed, is up a minor road off the A481 at Hundred House. It is perched on a small hump and looks as if it has been there forever. Inside the odd-shaped door at the end of the large porch there are seats in the nave for 22, no east window and only a door and a tiny slit window at the west end. The wooden bell tower sits near the end of the gable, without making the church look top-heavy, as does Croft in Herefordshire. The yew tree that once stood outside the east wall had collapsed in the winter of 1983 and the stump-hollow seems to be used for plastic water bottles. The north window has a triple curved top as if it was once three lights. The circular cross on top of the bell tower and the roof, repaired in 1961-2 has the roof beams projecting through the south wall.

Rhulen, which once had a pub, carpenter, shoemaker, blacksmith, shop and even a mat-maker, now has nothing but its woodland charm. It has a service twice a month on the second and fourth Sundays. The little guide book encourages visitors to see the slightly larger churches nearby at Cregrina and Glascwm, both of which have separate chancels (St David, Cregrina, is on p.88).

72 Chancel window, St David, Rhulen. © *B. Lowry*

St Mary the Virgin, Snead (Montgomeryshire)

Tucked away at the end of an orchard off the A489 near to Bishops Castle, Snead church comes under Hereford Diocese although it is firmly in Wales. It is easy to miss as there is no sign of it from the road and it involves a, sometimes wet, walk down a grassy path beside an orchard.

Most of the church dates from 1870, with only the lower part of the walls and north and south doorways being medieval. There is a new floor in the nave, which seats about 30, and unusually a new hatchment on the south side of the unplastered walls. This is showing the Morgan-Owen coat of arms – a married man with surviving wife (see colour plate 20).

The font is circular, twelfth century and has two handle-type projections. There is a nineteenth-century screen. The Augustinian Priory of Chirbury, Shropshire, was first set up in Snead but no sign of it remains.

Snead is usually open and services are held once a month (fourth Sundays).

APPENDIX 1

THE FRIENDS OF FRIENDLESS CHURCHES

The Friends of Friendless Churches, founded in 1957, exists to save churches and chapels of historic and architectural interest threatened by demolition or unseemly conversion.

Increasingly in recent years they have had to assume direct responsibility for such buildings and they now own, by freehold or by lease, 38 former churches including 18 in Wales. All of these faced certain decay or demolition prior to the Friends' intervention. In addition to those churches which are directly held by the Friends, the organisation has been responsible for saving over 100 more, many of which have subsequently been vested in the care of The Churches Conservation Trust established by Act of Parliament in 1969.

The Friends is an almost wholly voluntary organisation. It works in partnership with the Ancient Monuments Society with which it operates a joint membership scheme. It also administers two Trusts; one (called the Cottam Will Trust) for the purchase of objects of beauty to be placed in ancient Gothic churches for the furtherance of religion, and a second to benefit the three churches at Tilbury juxta Clare and Ovington in Essex and St Stephen in Bournemouth. It also holds funds on behalf of the churches of Llangua on the Welsh/English border, Besselsleigh in Berkshire, Long Crichel in Dorset and Eglwys Brewis in Glamorgan.

The Society is recognised as the equivalent in Wales of the Churches Conservation Trust – the remit of which covers only England – and is thus paid 100 per cent of the costs of taking Welsh churches into care, that cost being met in the proportion of 70 per cent from the state (through Cadw) and 30 per cent from the Church in Wales.

For more information, contact the Hon. Director, FFC, St Anne's Vestry Hall, 2 Church Entry, London EC4V 5HB. New members are welcome.

The following are brief descriptions of the churches belonging to the Friends, most of which are too large for inclusion in this book. They are usually unlocked or the key is kept close by a local keyholder. All are important architecturally and seven of them are included in the main text of this book.

St Andrew, Bayvil – (see pp.60-1)

St Mark, Brithdir, Gwynedd — An Arts & Crafts church a few miles east of Dolgellau, St Mark's was constructed by Henry Wilson between 1895-7. It has an unusual altar and font and some wonderful carvings of small animals on the pews.

St Mary, Derwen, Clwyd — This village church is famous for its screen, which, unlike Llanbabo, has pierced tracery panels so the congregation can see and hear what is going on in the chancel. There is a vine pattern on the bressumer. The font and cover date from Charles II (1665) and there is a fine churchyard cross in the circular churchyard. The lychgate has been incorporated into another building and the loft above it was once used as a school.

Hodgeston, Pembrokeshire (No dedication) — A large village church with a very fine medieval sedilia with triple arches and ogee-shaped canopies, also a double piscina of equal high quality. In 1856 David Brandon constructed a new east window and a new arch-braced roof that was heavily criticised at the time. In the chancel are heraldic tiles depicting the arms of the Rev. Thomas who had them installed.

St Peulan, Llanbeulan, Anglesey — (see p.22)

St Ellyw, Llanelieu, Talgarth, Powys — (with a beautiful medieval screen) (see p.97)

St Jerome, Llangwm Uchaf, Monmouthshire – is the newest venture, a large church restored by Seddon.

St Baglan, Llanfaglan, Caernarvon (Gwynedd) — A remote church in a walled enclosure close to the sea, too large to include.

St Mary, Llanfair Kilgeddin, Usk, Monmouthshire — A Victorian church by the river, too large to include, but worth a visit to see the Sedding reconstruction with graffito wall decoration by Heywood Sumner, which involves the top layer of plaster being cut back to reveal the decoration – the Creation.

St Figel, Llanfigael – as from Jan. 2007, vested in the Friends (see p.24)

St David, Llangeview, Monmouthshire — (see p.54)

Sss Afran, Euan and Sannen, Llantrisant, Anglesey — An L-shaped church in a field. It has a good range of eighteenth-century fittings and a good quality eighteenth-century tablet. To reach the building we had to walk (ten of us) over a steep style through some inquisitive cattle and then horses and only nine arrived. One retired defeated. However, it was worth the visit and who needs church wardens when you have four-footed ones. Afran, Euan and Sannen would have been pleased.

St David, Manordeifi, Pembrokeshire — An interesting church with a long nave, box pews and coracle, too large to include.

St Beuno, Penmorfa, Gwynedd – A small church with combined nave and chancel although with a screen. It is mainly fourteenth century with porch and vestry added in the eighteenth century. In 1880, the Victorians took away the gallery to make altar rails and seats. The lychgate is a nineteenth-century reconstruction of the earlier one and has a tablet in Welsh of 1698. The church is kept locked. The approach is difficult for disabled persons.

St Mary, Tal-y-Llyn, Anglesey — (see p.27)

St Cynhaearn, Ynyscynhaearn, Gwynedd — Built in 1832, it has a triple-decker pulpit, singers' gallery and fine stained glass by Powell of Whitefriars (1908). This is kept locked.

For further information, see: www.friendsoffriendlesschurches.org.uk

APPENDIX II
WELSH RELIGIOUS BUILDINGS TRUST

(YMDDIRIEDOLAETH ADDOLDAI CYMRU)

For further details of this trust, which was established in the 1990s, contact the Trust Manager, 10 Heol y Dwr, Penygroes, Caernarfon, Gwynedd LL54 6LR.

CONSERVING AND PROMOTING THE RELIGIOUS BUILT HERITAGE OF WALES

The Welsh Religious Buildings Trust has been set up to address some of the serious problems facing our rich inheritance of religious buildings. Some of our prime historical assets will be protected for future generations in the hands of the Trust, whilst the Trust will also serve as a focal point for dealing with the many problems that face those responsible for caring for the built religious heritage of Wales.

BACKGROUND

In May 1993, the Welsh Affairs Committee of the House of Commons recommended the setting up of a Redundant Churches and Chapels Fund for Wales. In 1994, a working party, sponsored by Cadw, was formed to review redundant historic chapels and their future. The resulting report, 'Redundant Historic Chapels in Wales' (September 1996), recommended the setting up of a new body – an independent charitable trust – to hold redundant historic chapels of significance for future generations and be an advisory body and information source.

The Trust has received funding from a variety of sources including Cadw, the Heritage Lottery Fund, The Architectural Heritage Fund, the Pilgrim Trust, Local Authorities and other donations.

AIMS AND OBJECTIVES

The aim of the Trust is to promote and advance the religious and associated heritage of Wales by:
- acquiring redundant religious buildings of significance and ensuring their conservation to the highest standards.
- providing advice and information to those owning or responsible for chapels and other historic religious buildings, and to other interested parties.

ACQUIRING BUILDINGS

The Trust seeks to acquire, as an owner of last resort, a limited number of redundant historic religious buildings. The scale of activities will be governed by three main factors:
- the number of buildings that fulfil the Trust's acquisition criteria.
- the number of buildings offered to the Trust for acquisition.
- the resources and funding available to the Trust.

The Trust intends to acquire at least one building per year, which will be repaired and conserved, and will be open to visitors with a programme of appropriate activities drawn up, according to the building's type and location. Local support for any held buildings is essential, and the local community will be invited to form active local committees or support groups.

ACQUISITIONS

The Trust's first acquisition is Libanus, a redundant Baptist Chapel at Waunclyndaf near Llansadwrn, Carmarthenshire. It is listed at II*, and is an unusually early example of a rural, gable-fronted two-storey chapel with a fine and little-altered interior with original furnishings. The Trust has other buildings including He-Dy-Cwrdd at Trecynon near Aberdare, a Grade II redundant Unitarian Chapel, Beili Du, a redundant Grade II Presbyterian Church of Wales chapel at Pentrebach near Sennybridge. The Trust has also obtained the chapel of Bethania (Baptist) Grade II*, at Maesteg.

RESEARCH AND INFORMATION

Many of those owning or responsible for historic buildings in Wales have an urgent need for advice, information and help, whether the building is still in use as a place of worship or is being used for other purposes. The Trust has therefore also been established with the intention of becoming an advisory body and a source of information to provide recommendations regarding funding, planning and conservation matters and possible new uses for buildings. The exact level and type of service provided will depend on the resources secured by the Trust.

APPENDIX III

THE ROUND TOWER CHURCHES SOCIETY

There are only two round tower churches in Wales, which are Llandysilio, St Tysilio in Powys (Montgomeryshire) and Bettwys Penpont church also in Powys (Breconshire). Both date from the 1860s and are not included as they are too large.

The Society has about 600 members from all over the world and gives grants to round tower churches and runs tours in the summer to see them. Most of them are in East Anglia.

For further details about the Society, contact the Hon. Secretary:
Mrs Lyn Stilgoe
Crabbe Hall, Burnham Market
King's Lynn
Norfolk PE31 8EN

APPENDIX IV
THE OPEN CHURCHES TRUST

The Open Churches Trust was created to try and reverse the trend to lock all churches between services. The need for many people to find a haven for peaceful prayer and reflection makes churches a useful asset for the community. Add to this the increased mobility of curious visitors who want to see the assets that would be otherwise hidden to all but local congregations, then one can understand their concerns. The Trust has now closed, but its Handbook is still available, and its work is in the hands of the Really Useful Group.

In Wales they have helped Churches Tourism Network Wales and the following churches have been helped to stay open:

Llanrwst, St Grwst
Llandysilio, St Tysilio (See Round Tower Society)
Milford Haven, St David
Pembroke, St Mary the Virgin
Penarth, St Augustine
Redwick, St Thomas the Apostle
Undy, St Mary the Virgin
Wrexham, St Giles

For further information, contact:
Brig. A.B.D. Gordon
The Really Useful Group Ltd
17 Slingsby Place
London
WC2E 9AB
Website: www.reallyuseful.com

APPENDIX V
SAINTS AND STONES GROUP

Nearly 1500 years ago the first Christian Pilgrims travelled the western sea routes, which led from Mediterranean Europe through Brittany and Cornwall to Pembrokeshire and Ireland. Many of these early saints – usually scions of the princely families of Brittany, Ireland and Wales, had journeyed far and wide, even to Rome or Jerusalem in their search for spiritual fulfilment before settling in north Pembrokeshire to establish religious houses and mission stations within the context of the social structure of west Wales in the sixth century.

Men like St David, St Brynach, St Justinian, St Teilo, St Colman, St Hywel and St Gwyndaf and even, briefly, St Patric, arrived in Pembrokeshire. Those who stayed founded their communities as Clas churches, gathering around themselves disciples and converts to the Christian church. These converts proclaimed their new allegiance in memorial stones dated from the fifth to the tenth centuries, which are found throughout north Pembrokeshire. Even in their own day these saints were revered and admired for their devotion and energetic promulgation of Christianity. From infancy they were credited with miraculous powers and the story of their lives became an integral part of the religious heritage of the early church in the west. Their saintly exploits were recorded during the eleventh and subsequent centuries with an immediacy which emphasises how fresh and relevant these figures were to contemporary society.

The Saints and Stones trails have been set up to give both holiday visitors and residents in the county access to some of Pembrokeshire's more remote and beautiful corners and to the deep spiritual qualities of these ancient places of worship. In July 1995 the first Saints and Stones trail was launched by Bishop Ivor Rees, with the backing of Menter Preseli and the EU leader programme II. In 1996 the project received a Commended in the Schroder Tourism Award. At Eastertide 1998 the Shadow of the Preselis trail was launched, led by Bishop Huw Jones. During Lent in 1999, supported by both Bishop Huw and Bishop Ivor, a third route, The Bishop's Road, was begun, following the old roads from the Bishop's palace at Llawhaden to St David's.

All three trails are focused on St David and the sacred landscape of the peninsula dedicated to him.

At least once every year, pilgrims gather at different churches along the three trails for worship and meditation and travel the lanes and byways by car or on foot to meet up for a communal lunch. In the afternoon there are guided visits to other churches along the way, tea, and finally a special welcome in the cathedral. It is particularly uplifting to arrive, after hours on the road or across country, often in drenching rain in the company of 30-40 fellow pilgrims, to participate in the simple words of a traditional evensong. The main event usually takes place each August but a variety of activities involving both visitors and local children and grown ups are arranged at other times.

Pilgrimages and visits to these churches continue all through the year. All the churches are open during daylight hours. The churches are not 'manned' but visitors are invited to sign the visitors' books and to enjoy their simplicity and atmosphere of peace and devotion.

For more information about the Saints and Stones Group, contact A. Eastham, Dolau, Dwrbach, Fishguard, SA65 9RN, who is one of the authors of *Saints and Stones* (Gomer 2002).

Activities since 2002 have increased, and the Group is now associated with St David's Tourism team and are planning to bring together local pilgrim routes across Wales, and to increase the use of churches and provide small group accommodation for visitors.

APPENDIX VI
THE HISTORIC CHURCHES SURVEY DATABASE

For four years between 1995 and 1999, Cadw sponsored the Welsh Archaeological Trusts to carry out a survey of 980 historic churches in Wales. The reports have not been published but Powys and Clywd have joined forces and their reports are available at www.cpat.org.uk and are divided into the following areas:

Brecknockshire Churches Survey
Denbighshire Churches Survey
Eastern Conwy Churches Survey
Flintshire Churches Survey
Montgomeryshire Churches Survey
Radnorshire Churches Survey
Wrexham Churches Survey

For further details, contact Mr R. Sylvester, 7a Church St, Welshpool, Powys SY21 7DL (01938 553670).

These surveys are very thorough (Pennant Melangell's report covers nine A4 pages) but they are purely archaeological and do not contain details about church contents, details of saints etc. which are contained in this book.

APPENDIX VII
ST DEINIOL'S LIBRARY, CLWYD

Daniel or Deiniol in Welsh has no connection to the Daniel of the den of lions. He was a monk who lived c.AD 500-584 and a descendant of the Celtic chieftain, Coel Godebog. He founded the monasteries of Bangor Fawr on the Menai Straits – Bangor Cathedral is dedicated to him – and Bangor Iscoed in Clywd (south-east of Wrexham).

According to Bede, the latter was the most famous monastery in Britain, but over 1000 monks were killed by Aethelfrith, King of Northumbria, at the battle of Chester. The monastery was destroyed so completely that its original site is uncertain. Deiniol was made the first Bishop of Bangor and there are two churches dedicated to him in Flintshire–Worthenbury and, of course, Hawarden. In Monmouthshire, Itton church (once called Llendeiniol) is dedicated to him and there are two other churches near Bala. At the Synod of Breifi (AD 545) it was Deiniol who persuaded David to attend so the two must have been friends, and in 546 Hawarden church was founded which today, rebuilt after a great fire in 1857, is closely associated with Prime Minister Gladstone and his large family. His second son was rector here (1872-1904) and there is a large memorial chapel to W.E. and his wife Catherine dating from 1906.

Before he retired, Gladstone, who lived in the Victorian castle opposite the church, had an idea which stemmed from his visit to Edward Pusey's funeral at Oxford. Pusey had established a memorial library leaving all his religious book collection to the formation of a college in Oxford to be the centre of 'religious faith, learning and personal sympathy' with Charles Gore as the first librarian. Gladstone determined to follow suit at Hawarden. An iron building was put up next to Hawarden church and by October 1880 bookcases with 22-24,000 volumes were in place. The first Warden was Rev. Gilbert Joyce and the old man put in £42,000 before his death in 1898 so that John Douglas, the architect, could build the present building which was completed in 1904 with bedrooms, refectory and a small chapel (25ft x 20ft) where there is a daily 8.00am service, sometimes in Welsh. There is just enough space for 20 people. The first service I attended used the Welsh Prayer Book and, as the priest stood at the back, the man next to me kept losing the place. It was only afterwards he told me he was a bishop and had a minion to turn pages for him.

There is nowhere like St Deiniol's; it is not a hotel or a college but a library with accommodation. Where else can you thumb through a former Prime Minister's books? Some have his handwritten notes in them – one of my friends researching Lord Curzon found no less than eight biographies of him to consult. It is a bibliophile's paradise.

The library has since been renamed the Gladstone Library and runs a variety of courses throughout the year. For further information contact the library website: www.gladstoneslibrary.org or phone 01244 532350.

GLOSSARY OF TERMS

Appliqué – Ornamental work where fabric is cut out and applied to the surface of other material

Apse – Semi-circular or polygonal recess often used as a chancel (see Pennant Melangell)

Apsidal – In the curved form of an apse

Auditory Church – One designed so congregation can hear the preacher

Baptistery – That part of the church in which baptism takes place

Berm – A broad base to a wall (see Llangelynn, St Caelynnin)

Board Bell Turret – Bell turret clad in wooden boards

Box Pew – A pew boxed in for keeping out draughts. Some have their own fireplaces

Bressumer – A carved horizontal beam used for supporting a screen (see St Anno, Llananno and Bettws Newydd)

Broach Spire – A spire, usually octagonal, rising from a square tower. The triangular face created is the 'broach'

Buttress – Can be angle (at each angle of the church), clasping (all round the corner), set back (near corners), diagonal (going out at angles from corners) or flying (as at St Paul's Cathedral)

Cell-y-Bedd – A cell with a grave, as at both Partrishow and Pennant Melangell. The former is west of the nave and the latter is in the apse and was rebuilt in 1900 on twelfth-century foundations. At the time post holes of an earlier building were discovered

Celure – Enriched area of roof above rood altar

Chapel – Sacred buildings less than churches. A Chapel of Ease was constructed for the comfort and ease of those living some distance from their parish church. Some have since become parish churches in their own right. A Chantry Chapel was one where the founder provided money for prayers to be said for his soul and that of his family in perpetuity. Mortuary Chapels are usually located in a graveyard

Clas Church – A pre-Norman church community

Collar Beam Roof – A cross beam, higher than a tie beam, across the apex of a roof

Communion Rails – After the Reformation these were used to keep stray dogs and other animals away from the altar

Consecration Cross – A cross incised in a circle, often painted red, to keep demons out of the church, usually put there when the church was consecrated

Corbel – Projection of stone, brick or wood used to support a beam, screen etc. It can be decorated with a face (see St Dogfael, Meline)

Easter Sepulchre – A place for the sacrament to be kept, usually on the north side of the chancel, from Good Friday until Easter Sunday

Family Pew – A box pew, sometimes with a fireplace and special furnishing where the squire or local nobleman sat during a service (see St Figel, Llanfigel)

Hatchments – A shield of arms acting as a memorial board found hanging on a church wall. This was common in Victorian days but unusual today. For a husband's death (wife surviving) the left half of the diagonal shield would be black, the wife's death (right side black) left white if the husband survives. Hatchments for widows, widowers, bachelors and spinster are all black and they get more complex if a second wife (or husband) survives (for a modern hatchment, see Snead, St Mary)

Keeil – Small stone-built rectangular chapels, mostly in ruins, in the Isle of Man. Churches are often built on their sites
Kempe Window – Windows made by Kempe – a famous Victorian stained-glass maker
King Post – A central vertical post on a tie beam supporting the roof

Label Stop – A carved face or corbel at the end of a rib
Llan – A church enclosure
Lychgate (or lich-gate) – From the Old English 'Lich' meaning 'corpse' and referring to the roofed gate of a churchyard. At Llangar there is a large lychgate for mourners and for coffins and the funeral service starts from the gate

Memento Mori – A death image (usually a skeleton) (see Partrishow, St Issui and Colva, St David)
Misericord – A hinged wooden seat which when tipped up forms a projection for the sitter to rest on when standing up. They are usually carved with heraldic beasts
Mullion – Vertical divide between lights (glass panels) of a window

Ogee Cap – Cap with S-shaped curve, sometimes used at the top of a monument
Oratory – Place of worship other than a church or chapel. A private chapel in a house is often called an Oratory
Ossuary – A place for storing bones (see Angle, Fishermen's Chapel)

Parclose Screen – A screen between a side chapel and another part of the church
Parish – From the Anglo-Saxon word 'parochium', the parish is the smallest unit of ecclesiastical administration. For more information, read A. Jones, *A Thousand Years of the English Parish* (Windrush Press, 2000)
Parvis – Used as the name of the room above the porch
Piscina – Recess for washing holy vessels with basin and drain
Porticus – Side chapel or porch-like chamber entered from the main body of the church
Preaching Cross – A cross outside the church used for preaching in the open air
Premonstratensian – White order of canons belonging to order founded in 1120 by St Norbert at Prémontré, France
Priest Holes – Hiding places dating from late 16th century in castles and large houses for Roman Catholic priests to hide from the law. Harkington Hall, Worcestershire has at least four.

Quatrefoil – Figure with four radiating petals. They can be an edge to heraldic shields on a tomb

Reredos – Decorative screen behind and above an altar

Retable – A reredos (screen at the back of the altar) with painted panels, often made of material, and quite scarce today

Rood Loft – A platform above the rood screen, often elaborately carved and used by singers or musicians. Most removed at the Reformation (see St Anno, Llananno)

Rood Screen – Decorative screen separating chancel from nave, usually built to support a rood loft, above which was the Great Rood – a crucifixion group of the Virgin, Christ and St John the Apostle. They were removed at the Reformation

Round Tower Churches – Common in East Anglia. For details, see the excellent publications of the Round Tower Churches Society, 6 The Warren, Old Catton, Norwich NR6 7NW

Saddleback – Tower with a gabled roof resembling a saddle (see St Madoc, Llanmadoc, Glamorgan)

Sounding Board – A board above the lectern to improve the sound

Squint (or Hagioscope) – A hole cut through masonry, usually at an oblique angle so that the subsidiary priest could see the High Altar

Scratch Dials – (Also known as 'Mass Dials'.) A sundial, often crudely scratched, on the south wall of a church to indicate the time of Mass, often 9.00am

Stoup – A holy water basin, often in the porch

Terrier – An inventory

Tie Beam Roof – A roof with timbers crossing horizontally from one side of the base of the roof to the other and connecting the feet of rafters

Tympanum – Space enclosed between a lintel and the arch above. Often elaborately carved and over the south door (see Llanllywel, St Llwyel)

Verger – Originally official responsible for carrying the 'verge' or mace. Now used for the person responsible for the interior fabric of the church

Wagon Roof – A curved interior roof that looks like the inside of a wagon

WELSH GLOSSARY

Abad	Abbot
Abaty	Abbey
Aber	estuary
Afon	river
Argoed	wood or grove
Bach	small
Bedd	grave
Bedigaid	blessed
Betwys	chapel
Brith	speckled
Bwlch	gap
Carreg	stone or rock
Cau	hollow or enclosed
Clawdd (pl. Cloddiau)	ditch or hedge
Coch	red
Congli	corner
Cwrt	court, yard
Derwen	oak
Diffwys	precipice or abyss
Dol (pl. Dolau)	meadow
Dyffryn	valley
Eglwys	church
Eisteddfa	seat, resting place
Erw	acre
Esgob	bishop
Ffald	sheepfold, pen or run
Ffordd	way, road
Ffrwd	stream, torrent
Gardd (pl. gerddi)	enclosure or fold into which calves were first turned
Glas	green
Gogof	cave
Gorffwysfa	resting place
Gris	step
Gwastad	plain
Gwaun	moor, mountain, meadow

Gwely	bed, resting place
Gwynt	wind
Hafn	gorge, ravine
Hafod	summer dwelling
Hen	old
Heol	street, road
Hir	long
Isaf	lower or lowest
Isel	low
Llan	church, monastery or enclosure
Llanbedr	St Peter's church
Llanddewi	St David's church
Llanfair	St Mary's church
Llanfihangel	St Michael's church
Llanerch	clearing, glade
Llidiard	gate
Llwch (pl. Llychau)	lake
Llwd	grey
Llyn	lake
Lon	road, lane
Maen	stone
Maenor	stone-built house for chieftain or rich land surrounding it
Maerdref	hamlet
Maes	open field
March	horse
Marchog	knight
Marian	gravel
Mawnog	peat bog
Mawr	great or big
Melyn	yellow
Moel	bare hill
Mur	wall
Mynach	monk
Mynachdy	monastic grange
Mynwent	churchyard
Mynydd	mountain, moorland
Nant	brook
Neuadd	hall
Newydd	new
Noddfa	hospice
Nyth	nest
Oen	lamb
Offeiriad	priest
Pandy	fulling-mill
Pant	hollow, valley
Pen (pl. pennau)	head, top, end, edge
Penrhyn	promontory
Pensaer	architect
Pentref	homestead
Person	parson
Pistyll	spout or waterfall

Plas	seat of gentleman
Plwyf	parish
Pwll	pit or pool
Rhaeadr	waterfall
Rhiw	hill or slope
Rhos	moor or promontory
Rhyd	ford
Saeth	arrow
Sant (pl. San)	saint; saint or monk
Sarn (pl. Sarnau)	causeway
Simnai (pl. Simdde)	chimney
Swydd	seat, lordship, office
Sych	dry
Tai or Ty (pl. tai)	house
Talwrn	exposed hillside, open space, threshing floor, cockpit
Tan	under
Teg	fair
Tir	land or territory
Tom or tomen (Tump in Herefordshire)	mound
Ton (pl. tonnau)	lea or grassland
Torglwyd	gate or door-hurdle
Towyn or Tywyn	sea shore
Traen	third part
Traeth	strand or shore
Traws	cross
Tref	homestead or hamlet
Tros	over
Trwyn	nose, point or cape
Twyr	tower
Twyn	hillock, knock
Tyddyn	small farm or holding
Uchaf	highest
Uchel	high
Uwch	above, over
Wyn	lamb (see 'oen')
Ynys (pl. ynysoedd)	island
Ysbyty	hospital, hospice
Ysgol	school
Ysgubor	barn
Ystafell	chamber, hiding-place
Ystrad	valley, holm or river meadow

BIBLIOGRAPHY

Bangor Diocese, *Directory of Open Churches* (2003)
Barber, C., *Exploring Kilvert Country* (Abergavenny, 2003)
Beverton, T.D., *The Book of Welsh Saints* (Cambridge, 2000)
Bushel, Rev. W., *Caldey – An Island of the Saints* (Arch. Camb, 1968)
CADW (Yates, N), *Rug, Llangar & Gwydir Uchaf, Combined Guidebook* (Cardiff, 2003)
Corbett, J., *Castles in the Air* (Gwydir, London, 2005)
Crossley and Ridgway, *Screens, Lofts and Stalls of Monmouthshire* (Newport, 1965)
Davies, Rev. D., *The Ancient Celtic Church of Wales* (London, 1910)
Davies, D.W. and Eastham, A., *Saints and Stones* (Llandysul, 2002)
Davis, P. and Lloyd-Fern, S., *Lost Churches of Wales & the Marches* (Stroud, 1990)
Edward, T., *The Face of Wales* (London, 1950)
Gregory, D., *Radnorshire – a Historical Guide* (Llanrwst, 1994)
Guy, J. and Smith, E., *Ancient Gwent Churches* (Newport, 1979)
John, B., *Pembrokeshire* (Newton Abbot, 1979)
Kinross, J., *Fishguard Fiasco* (Tenby, 1974; reprinted Almeley, Hereford, 2007)
Kinross, J., *Walking & Exploring the Battlefields of Britain* (Newton Abbott, 1988)
McAsey, J., *Ancient Chapels & Churches of Wales* (Talybont, 2003)
Massingham, H., *The Southern Marches* (London, 1952)
Owen, E., *The Later Life of Bishop Owen* (Llandysul, 1961)
Pevsner, Sir Nikolaus, *The Buildings of England*
    Haslam, *Powys* (Brecon, Montgomery & Radnor) (London, 1979)
    Hubbard, *Clwyd* (Denbigh & Flint) (London, 1986)
    Lloyd, Orbach & Scourfield, *Pembrokeshire* (London, 2004)
    Newman, *Glamorgan* (London, 1995)
    Newman, *Gwent* (Monmouthshire) (London, 2000)
Plomer, W., *Diary of Francis Kilvert* (London, 1944)
Rees, N. and John, T. *Pilgrimage: A Welsh Perspective* (Llandysul, 2002)
Salter, M., *Old Parish Churches of Gwent, Glamorgan & Gower* (Malvern, 2002)
Salter, M., *Old Parish Churches of North Wales* (Malvern, 1993)
Salter, M., *Old Parish Churches of Mid-Wales* (Malvern, 2003)
Salter, M., *Old Parish Churches of South West Wales* (Malvern, 2003)

INDEX OF CHURCHES BY PLACE NAME

Alltmawr, St Mauritius 74
Angle, Fishermen's Chapel 60
Arthog, St Catherine 45

Bayvil, St Andrew 60-1
Bettws Chapel, Holy Trinity 75-7
Bettws Newydd (no dedication) 51-2

Caldey Island, St David 63
Capel-y-Ffin, St 74, 78–9
Cascob, St Michael 74, 79-83
Cefnllys, St Michael 74, 83-5
Colva, St David 74, 85-8
Cregrina, St David 74, 88-90
Crinow, St Teilo 60, 64-5

Dolobran, Friends Meeting House 74, 90-1

Echo, Colva 88
Efenechtyd, St Michael & All Angels 33-5

Kemeys Commander, All Saints 51–3
Kilgrrwg, Holy Cross 51, 53

Little Newcastle, St Peter 60, 65–6
Llananno, St Anno 74, 91–2
Llanbabo, St Pabo 21-2
Llanbadarn-y-Garreg, St Padarn 74, 92-3
Llanbeulan, St Peulan 22-4
Llandanwg, St Tanwg 45-6
Llandeilo Tal-y-Bont, St Teilo (St Fagans) 37-8

Llandeloy, St Eloi 60, 66–7
Llanddewi Fach, St David 74, 94-5
Llanelieu, St Ellyw 74, 96-7
Llanfaelog, St Maelog 21, 25
Llanfaelrhys Rhiw, St Maelrhys 45–6
Llanfigel, St Figel 21, 24–5
Llangar, All Saints 31-2, 45
Llangelynn, St Caelynnin 45, 47–8
Llangeview, St David 51, 54-6
Llangwyfan, St Cwyfan 21, 25
Llangua, St James 51, 56-8
Llanhowel, St Hywel 67–8
Llanlychan, St Hychan 35, 36-7
Llanina, St Ina 29–30
Llanllywel, St Llywel 51, 58-9
Llanmadoc, St Madoc (Gower) 38-40
Llanmihangel, St Michael & All Angels 40-1
Llanrwst, Gwydir Uchaf Chapel 31, 45, 49
Lanstinan, St Justinian 60, 68-9
Llanwnda, St Gwyndaf 60, 70-1

Meline, St Dogfael 60, 71-2
Menai Bridge, St Tysilio 21, 25-6
Mounton, St Andomenus 51, 59–60
Mwnt, Holy Cross 29-31

Partrishow, St Issui 74, 97-9
Pennant Melangell, St Melangell 74, 99-100
Penmynydd, St Gredifael 21, 26–7
Pilleth, St Mary 74, 100-1
Pistyll, St Beuno 45, 50
Porthkerry, St Curig 37, 41

INDEX OF CHURCHES BY PLACE NAME

Rhos-on-Sea, St Trillo 31, 37
Rhulen, St David 74, 102-3
Rug Chapel 31, 45

St Davids, Our Lady & St Non Chapel 60, 72-3
St Donat, St Donats 42-3

St Govan's Chapel 60, 62-3
Snead, St Mary the Virgin 74, 104

Tal-y-llyn, St Mary 27-8
Tin Churches (Swansea St Anne) 44

Y-Strad-Ffin, St Paulinus 28–9

GENERAL INDEX

Abberfraw 25
Abracadabra Charm 82
Advestus (son of Guanus) 38
Aeddan 51
Afran, St (with St Ieuan & St Sanan) 28
Aidan, Saint 38, 71
Aircol Lawhir, King 58
Alice Springs golf course (Wales) 51
Allen, Blanche 64
Alternun, Cornwall 72
Ancient Celtic Church of Wales, The 82
Angers Cathedral 97
Arthur, King 21
Atlantic College 42
Attlee, Clement 35
Aubrey family 97
Aurelian, Paul 29

Baily, Theodore 64
Baker, Arthur 35
Baldwin of Brecon 97
Bangor (by Menai) 21
Bardsey Island 45, 47
Barker 65
Barnes, Rev 68
Barti Ddu (Pirate) 66
Beaufort, Margaret 27
Bell, Reginald and Farrar 59
Berrington, Pilot Officer 51
Bevan of Glebe Farm 40

Bevan, Joseph & Fred 53
Blackamoor Inn 35
Black Legion, The 70
Bold, William 22
Boulton of Cheltenham 92
Bowen, Peter 41
Bradenstoke Priory 43
Breginton family 59
Bronwydd House 72
Brychan Brychenin 35
Bryngwyn 51
Bushell, Rev. 64

Cadfael, Brother 58
Cadw 25, 31-2
Caio 29
Caldey Cistercians 63
Caring for God's Acre 73
Camden 83
Carmarthen Museum 29
Carter, Coates 60, 64, 67
Caröe, W.D. 97
Cartwright of Aberedow 85
Cawdor, family 28, 70
Cheriton Pottery 40
Chirbury Priory 104
Civil War, The 42, 101
Clive Powell, Roger 61
Clyro 75, 94
Clytha 51
Collier, E.V. 68
Colva echo 88
Compostella 99
Conway family 35
Corbett, Judy 50

Creed 53
Crinow 60
Curr, Henrietta 45
Cyfyw, Saint 54
Cynan 26
Cynwyd 32

Davies, Rev. D. 83-5
Davies, Rev. J.D. 38-40
Davies, Rupert (Maigret) 50
Davies, Thos. 85
Deinol, Saint 21
Deorham, Battle of 38
Derwen, St Mary 35
Directory of Bangor Open Churches 21, 25
Dirinon, Brittany 72
Diserth (wart curing well) 25
Dog-tongs 24, 26
Dol, France 64
Dolphin, Mr (Pirate) 42
Domesday Book 79
Donatus, St 42
Dubricius, Saint 64
Dynawd Fyr 21

Edward Tudor 27
Edwards, John 65
Edwin family 41
Edw, River 88
Elcho, Lord and Lady 41
Ensic 38
Ethelred, King 30
Evill, Walter 59

GENERAL INDEX

Filwr, Gwynlliw 54
Fishguard Ferries 70
Fishguard Fiasco 66
Flemings 31
Forsyth (stained glass maker) 35
Friends of the Friendless Churches: 7, 9, 22, 27, 54, 61, 66-7, 96-7, 105-6

Gabb, Richard Baker 97
Garland, HMS 53
Garn Fawr Hillfort 71
Glasbury 94
Glastonbury Abbey 30
Gobham 63
Gower, The 38
Geoffrey of Monmoth 68
George VI, King 83
Gill, Eric 78-9
Glendower, Owen 100
Graham, Sir Crosland 35
Graig Olway 54
Grant, Griffith 41
Griffiths, Lewis 92
Guenhaf 38
Gwendoline, Saint, of Talgarth 97
Gwernsey 54
Gwydir Castle 42
Gwyddfarch 26

Hael of Llydaw 37
Halliday, G.E. 64
Haslam (see Pevsner)
Hearst, William Randolph 42-3
Heaton, R.B. 99
Helena, Empress 21-2
Hengoed 85
Henry VII (Duke of Richmond) 27
Hentland 38
Hergest, Rev J. 90
Holyhead 27
Hook Mason 101
Hundred House 102

Iddon 38
Ithon, River 83, 91

Jasper Tudor 27
Jickells, John 41
Jones, Dr (Breathaliser) 22

Jones & Wallis 25
Jones, W. 56

Keeil site 53
Kempson, F.R. 77
Kilvert, Rev. Francis 39, 77, 78, 88, 94
Knox, family of Llanstinan 68

Laud, Archbishop 32
Lavers & Barraud 72
Lawhir, Aircol 58
Letavia 92
Lewis, D. 92
Lewis, R. 65
Liddell VC, Capt. 60
Llandaff Cathedral 65
Llandeilo Fawr 65
Llandeilo Llwydarth 65
Llandewi Velfrey 64
Llangolman 65
Llangwym Uchaf, St Jerome 53
Llanmaes 40
Llanrhidian 38
Llanrwst 31
Llanwnog Church 91
Lloyd of Llanarth 29
Lloyd, Elizabeth 82
Lloyd, Ironfounders 90
Lloyd, Sir Thomas of Bronwydd 71
Llwyn Gwilym 77
Llwynygwril 45
Longcroft, Captain 30
Longsword, Ceri 41
Lourdes 99
Loveys, Caroline 65

Mabinogion, The 68
Macbeth 28
Maelgwyn 92
Maes-y-Groes 38
Manordeifi church 67, 106
Maredudd 27
Mathern 59
Mathias, R. 64
Maurice of Nassau 75
Mauritana 92
Maxentius 45
Maximinian, Emperor 75
Memento Mori 84, 86
Michael, St. 33

Miles, Rev H. 68
Monnow, River 36
Morgan-Owen family 104
Morris, Lewis 21
Morris Studios 72
Morrison, Sir Alec 78
Mortimer, Earl of 100
Mortimer's Cross, Battle of 27
Mungo, Saint 37

Nash, Mr 38
Newbery (glass designer and maker) 41, 53
Newtown School 91
Nicholson & Son 85

Ogle, Captain R.N. 66
Old Radnor church 85
Owen, Dr Robert 46
Owens, Sir John 68
Owens, Fanny 68

Padarn 38
Painscastle 74, 94
Pant y Phillip Estate 68
Pant-y-Polion 29
Parc Glas 64
Parkinson, A.J. 32
Paul-de-Leon, Saint 29
Paulinus of York 29
Pearce, Colin 25
Pearcey, Rev. P.A. 90
Penrice Castle 38
Peters, Ellis 58
Petran & Guean 92
Petrie, Flinders 64
Pevsner, Sir N. 59, 63, 71, 91, 97
Pilate's Wife (window) 32
Pontardulais 37
Pontrobert 90
Porthkerry Castle 41
Portreye, Reynold 41
Precious Bane 83
Price of Pilleth 101
Prichard John 94
Pringle family 68
Prudhomme, Charles 66

Ramsay Island 68
Rees, W. Jenkins 82
Rhoose Airport 41
Rhydspence Inn 75

Ridgway & Crossley 51, 54
Rycote St Michael, Oxon 32

Saint Fagan's Museum 37
Saint Margaret's 51
Salusbury, Theodora 53
Sandglan 37
Sarn Badrig Ridge 46
Seddon, J.P. 53, 94
Sellack 38
Senogles, David 26
Seven Deadly Sins 32-3
Shakespeare 100
Stones, Charles (carpenter) 79
Stradling family 42
Swallow, The 66
Swann, Bill 25
Swansea 38, 65
Swansea, St Anne's 44
Swansea, Brecon, Bishop of 101
Symons, Ann 66

Taf, River 65

Tate, Col. W. 70
Tate, Tiffany 25
Taylor, Thomas 45
Taylors of Loughborough 41
Tappers, W. J. 101
Teilo, St. 38, 64
Tethen, Baron 75
Thomas, David 72
Thomas, Lieut. 67
Thomas R.S. 46, 51
Thomas, Wheldon 21
Tin churches 44
Towyn 47
Trehowel Farm (Tate's HQ) 70-1
Trevethen, Baron 75
Tudor, Gronw 26
Tudor, Owen 27
Tyrwhitt family 42

Valley Airfield 24-5
Valois, Katherine de 27
Vespers 47
Voelcker, Adam 25

Waddington family 59

Walker of Liverpool 92
Walters, John 35
Watkins, Walter 97
Webb, Mary 83
Weedon, Bucks. 35
Weobley Castle 38
Wesley 41
West Kirby 61
Whitford Chapel, Devon 58
Whitland 29
Wildlife in churchyards 73
Williams, Coningsby 26
Williams & Fletcher 34
Williams, John (High Sheriff) 22
Williams, Morgan Stuart 42
Williams, Rowan, Archbishop 60
Withers, R.J. 71
Wood, Abram 47
Wolfe-Murray, Patricia 99
Wynn, Sir Richard 47

Ynyr, King 38
Yny-y-Moch (Pig Island) 26